"This book resonates with gospel clarity and gospel compassion. It will empower you to share the good news of Jesus with those who grapple with gender-identity issues. The book is smart, wise, persuasive, and practical." RUSSELL MOORE, President, the Southern Baptist Ethics and Religious Liberties Commission; author of *Onward*

"I have been waiting for a resource that would provide me with a clear, loving, and gospel-centered analysis on the topic of gender dysphoria, and I have finally found it. This resource will be incredibly helpful in assisting the body of Christ to be a light in today's cultural climate." JACKIE HILL PERRY, writer and artist

"Andrew T. Walker is one of the young bright lights in the evangelical church. Here, he helps the church both understand and compassionately respond to today's challenges on gender identity." RYAN T. ANDERSON, Senior Research Fellow, the Heritage Foundation

"The transgender debate is one that easily arouses passions on both 'sides.' With gospel clarity and Christ-like compassion, Andrew Walker skillfully navigates a path between folly and cruelty. In so doing, he helps us to see why the gospel of Jesus Christ is good news for the transgendered. I highly commend this clearheaded and warmhearted introduction to one of the most challenging issues of our time." ROB SMITH, lecturer in ethics, Sydney Missionary & Bible College

"Andrew Walker brings a sharp mind and pastoral heart to a complex and often painful issue, and the result is a hugely helpful resource for the church today, full of wisdom, grace and truth. I recommend it highly." SAM ALLBERRY, speaker with Ravi Zacharias International Ministries

"The post-Christian West says that we are what we think we are, not what our bodies reveal us to be—and this is one of the chief challenges to Christianity today. That is why *God and the Transgender Debate* is so important. It is a countercultural, compassionate, must-read book." DENNY BURK, President, the Council for Biblical Manhood and Womanhood

"This is exactly the book I have been longing for and praying that someone would write. Andrew T. Walker brings biblical clarity to a minefield of complexity and controversy. He sets out a clear pathway to help Christian leaders and all believers navigate tricky terrain with grace, gentleness and genuine love for transgender people." JONATHAN BERRY, D: ... Freedom Trust

"Walker has done what many could not. He has not only given the church a tool for greater understanding of this area, but has done so with grace, conviction, careful study and thought, and deep love for others. This is not only a timely book; it's a timeless resource for anyone desiring to serve and love their neighbor as themselves."

TRILLIA NEWBELL, author of *Enjoy* and *Fear and Faith*

"What should Christians think and say about those who feel their gender is out of line with their biological sex? Should we accept that or silently acquiesce? Andrew Walker rightly says no, but in a compassionate manner that recognizes the psychological struggles and the suffering of people who experience alienation from themselves as God made them."

ROBERT P. GEORGE, McCormick Professor of Jurisprudence, Princeton University

"Christians must begin to think and speak biblically, in truth and love, about this issue. Andrew Walker has provided a steady foundation from which the church can begin to grapple with this cultural shift."

KAREN SWALLOW PRIOR, author of *Fierce Convictions—The Extraordinary Life of Hannah More: Poet, Reformer, Abolitionist*

"This book combines an extraordinary range of attributes. It tackles a contemporary issue; it is marked by humanity and compassion; it respects the Bible; it is open and honest; it is full of Christ-like love; it is usefully practical; and it places the discussion in the context of the big picture of the Bible. It is a model for the open and sensitive discussion of many contemporary issues."

PETER ADAM, retired Principal of Ridley College, Melbourne, Australia

"This is an extremely important book, not just in Andrew Walker's practical treatment of the tricky and confusing topic of transgenderism, but in the very truthful and compassionate way he deals with it. This is really a book about how we love the gender-dysphoric person with the full grace and glorious truth of the gospel itself. It is a uniquely beautiful and very practical book. Absolutely 'Must-Read' material."

GLENN T. STANTON, Director of Family Formation Studies at Focus on the Family

"I am so pleased this excellent book has been published. Its biblical depth and sensitivity are well worth the price alone. The closing chapters are especially important regarding the role of the church, the effect on children and the resultant tough questions that arise."

COLIN BENNETT, Vice-Principal, Moorlands College, Hampshire, UK

"Gender-identity questions are among the most radical of our time—and the church is not prepared. Andrew T. Walker has thought deeply about these things, and is an invaluable guide for faithful Christians walking through the heat and confusion of this debate."

ROD DREHER, author of *The Benedict Option*

"The Bible says to love your neighbor and to do unto others as you would have them do unto you. How can Christians love our transgender neighbors compassionately, without compromising our faith? Andrew Walker puts us on the right path." ERICK ERICKSON, Editor, *The Resurgent*

"Andrew Walker's tender application of God's word to our muddled lives today should make this book one of the first places to turn for Christlike grace and truth as we seek to love all our neighbors as ourselves."

ED SHAW, author of *The Plausibility Problem*; co-founder of livingout.org

"This book puts the hand of the suffering into the hands of the Savior, and therefore, this is the book that I will put into the hands of parents struggling to know how God's word speaks into loving a child who struggles with gender-identity issues. In addition to its loving pastoral care and biblical family guidance, this book models how to discern the times, and to respond with Christian hope."

ROSARIA BUTTERFIELD, author of *Openness Unhindered* and *Secret Thoughts of an Unlikely Convert*

"Andrew T. Walker has written a book not about the debates but about people. It is clear, and clarifies matters in a way which will help us all."

PETER BARNES, Editor, *AP Magazine*, Australia

"Andrew Walker offers overdue clarity, compassion, and practical wisdom on one of the most difficult questions of our day. Along the way he demonstrates not only that we need not choose between truth and love, as we are often told, but that especially on these issues of human identity, we cannot. This is such an important book."

JOHN STONESTREET, President, the Colson Center for Christian Worldview

"One of evangelicalism's brightest young stars helps us understand how the gospel can be good news, and how the church can be a faithful community, for somebody experiencing gender dysphoria. If you are looking for a one-stop resource for responding biblically to questions about transgender and gender fluidity, look no further."

BRUCE RILEY ASHFORD, Provost and Professor of Theology and Culture, Southeastern Baptist Theological Seminary; author of *Every Square Inch*

"Topics like this require a mixture of compassion and clarity, and Andrew Walker writes with both. This is a hugely helpful introduction to a complex, controversial, and often painful subject."

ANDREW WILSON, Teaching Pastor, King's Church London;
author of *The Life We Never Expected*

"Andrew Walker's short book deals well with the emotional issues surrounding this difficult area, and is a kind and clear lesson in how to respond with godly love and wisdom. This book will help us all to care and counsel well."

SIMON MANCHESTER, Senior Minister, St Thomas North Sydney

"We need an extra measure of wisdom and an extra measure of compassion in walking with people who struggle with their gender identity. Andrew Walker demonstrates the kind of wisdom and compassion we will need in the days ahead."   TREVIN WAX, author of *This Is Our Time*

"This is both a resource for and a challenge to the church: a challenge to be compassionate, convictional and gracious communities where those suffering with gender dysphoria find hope in the gospel, grace in God's promises, and willing fellow travelers for the hard journey home."

DARREN MIDDLETON, Convener,
PCV Church and Nation Committee, Australia

"Andrew Walker writes on a tough subject with courage and compassion. This is the book Christians need to read to cut through the politically-correct noise and get to the heart of one of the most contentious issues of our time."   DAVID FRENCH, Senior Fellow, National Review Institute

"Andrew Walker has given us a much-needed resource for understanding the questions around transgender issues. With clarity and gentleness, he calls us back to a biblical vision of humanity, creation, and gender, and invites us to see fidelity to that vision as the most loving way we can engage with a confused world."

MIKE COSPER, Founder of Harbor Media; author of *The Stories We Tell*

Andrew T. Walker

GOD

and the

TRANSGENDER

DEBATE

**What Does the Bible Actually Say
About Gender Identity?**

thegoodbook
COMPANY

To Matt and Carey Murphy,
who have taught both my family and their community
what it means joyfully to follow Christ in broken bodies
amid a broken creation.

God and the Transgender Debate:
What Does the Bible Actually Say About Gender Identity?
© Andrew Walker, 2017

Published by:
The Good Book Company

Tel (US): 866 244 2165
Tel (UK): 0333 123 0880
Email (US): info@thegoodbook.com
Email (UK): info@thegoodbook.co.uk

Websites:
North America: www.thegoodbook.com
UK: www.thegoodbook.co.uk
Australia: www.thegoodbook.com.au
New Zealand: www.thegoodbook.co.nz

ISBN: 9781784981785 | Printed in Denmark

Design by André Parker

CONTENTS

FOREWORD

Dr R. Albert Mohler, Jr.

The Christian church in the West now faces a set of challenges that exceeds anything it has experienced in the past. The sexual revolution is fundamentally restructuring our culture's collective understanding of family, society, and the very meaning of life.

These challenges would be vexing enough for any generation. But the contours of our current challenge have to be understood as part of a larger project which is affecting every square inch of society. This revolution, like all revolutions, takes few prisoners. In other words, it demands total acceptance of its revolutionary claims and the affirmation of its aims. This is the problem now faced by Christians who are committed to uncompromising faithfulness to the Bible as the word of God, and to the gospel as the only message of salvation.

The crisis this revolution poses to the church of Jesus Christ is tantamount to the sort of theological challenges posed by the Trinitarian and Christological controversies of the early church, the Pelagian controversy faced by Augustine, or even the theological challenges faced by the Reformers themselves. In each of these controversies, the true church understood that it could not embrace any theological conviction which might undermine the central truths of the gospel. Even in the face of stiff cultural and political opposition, the faithful church has always recognized its call to hold fast to the faith once for all delivered to the saints (Jude 1 v 3).

Even more than the movement for the normalization of homosexuality, the transgender revolution challenges the most basic structures of society. Transgenderism disagrees with thousands of years of consensus regarding gender and human identity shared by almost every culture, including those not influenced by Christian morality. Now, for instance, some preschools in Europe prohibit the use of gendered pronouns, eradicating terms such as "girl" and "boy" from the schools' idiom. This example is one among many demonstrating why the transgender revolution raises questions that we cannot possibly avoid.

Moreover, the transgender revolution represents one of the most difficult pastoral challenges that churches in this generation will face. Just as churches include many people struggling with same-sex attraction, churches will be ministering to men and women struggling with gender confusion. This kind of confusion concerns the very core of our being, and cannot be pushed to the periphery of our consciousness. Our gender identity is fundamental to our self-knowledge. A biblical response to the transgender revolution will require the church to develop new skills of compassion and understanding as we encounter persons, both inside and outside our congregations, who are struggling.

The ideological assumptions driving the transgender revolution did not even exist until very recently. This revolution required certain epistemological and moral shifts in order for it to emerge as legitimate. Transgenderism is birthed out of Western society's challenges to the institution of marriage and out of the project of social revolutionaries to redefine sexuality and normalize same-sex relationships. These shifts deconstructed objective social norms and instead advocated a "social construction" of reality.

The reasons why Christians must confront the transgender revolution and why we must faithfully preach the gospel to transgender persons are because we love God and we love our neighbor. The sexual revolution is a failed experiment: one that will only result in personal tragedy and cultural chaos. The church should be a place of refuge for the casualties of the sexual revolution. We must point others to the redemption and healing found in the gospel of Christ. We must be a people who look to the gospel as we await the redemption of all things—including gender and sexuality—and the fulfillment of all of God's promises in Christ Jesus.

This book is the type of resource the church needs in these challenging times. Theologically careful and full of pastoral wisdom, Andrew not only unpacks the history and ideology of the transgender revolution; he also shows us how to respond faithfully to the challenges it poses with the gospel of Jesus Christ. This book should be in the hands of pastors, lay leaders, and church members everywhere.

The sexual revolution poses challenges that are not simply going to disappear. The church must be ready to meet these challenges with biblical fidelity and Christ-like compassion. The church must move forward, confident that the Scriptures are sufficient, clear, and have the power to transform broken lives. We must remember that Scripture gives God's people a comprehensive worldview which equips us to wrestle with even the most challenging ethical dilemmas of our time. Finally, we must hold fast to the gospel, knowing that it alone provides the only true remedy for all our troubles and struggles, and the only sure answer for all our questions and doubts.

Dr R. Albert Mohler, Jr.
President, Southern Baptist Theological
Seminary, Louisville, USA

1. HE HAD COMPASSION

Jesus debated issues. But much more than that, he loved people.

All kinds of people came to speak with him during his time on earth. The religious insiders. The socially excluded. The handicapped. The undesirables. The rich, the poor, the young, the old. Those whose lives had been messed up by others, and those whose lives had been messed up by themselves.

And Jesus loved them all, made time for them all, and respected them all. He didn't always agree with them (and he disagreed with the religious insiders more than anyone). But he always loved them—especially those who came to him hurting. In a lovely phrase taken from the prophet Isaiah and applied to himself, Jesus described his approach to them:

> *A bruised reed he will not break, and a smoldering wick he will not quench. (Matthew 12 v 20)*

The visual imagery Jesus uses is important to remember and beautiful to see. Jesus will not let fragile people crumble or collapse beneath the weight of their struggles. Jesus wants to take those who feel they are close to flickering out and help return them to brightness and warmth. Jesus is tender and gentle toward those who think they cannot go any further.

He described life with him as "rest," and invited the burdened to come and enjoy it:

> *Come to me, all who labor and are heavy laden, and I will give you rest. Take my yoke upon you, and learn from me, for I am gentle and lowly in heart, and you will find rest for your souls. For my yoke is easy, and my burden is light.*
> *(Matthew 11 v 28-30)*

So if you're reading this close to your breaking point, if you're feeling that your spark is very, very dim or that you're too broken to stand—or if you know someone who is in that situation—Jesus says, *I get that. I see that. I love you, and I want to help. I may not always agree with you, but I will only disagree with you because I want the best for you. I've come to stiffen you, not to snap you. I don't snuff out flickering candles. I want to fan them into flames.*

Jesus loved people. That's important for me to remember as I write a book with the word "debate" in its title. And it's good for you to remember as you read a book with the word "transgender" in its title. Because at its heart, this debate isn't about a debate. It's about people: precious people made in the image of God who are hurting, who are confused, who are angry, who are scared, who may have been told by their family that they are unwelcome. It's about some people who are delighted with how culture has shifted when it comes to gender identity, and other people who are concerned about how culture has shifted.

What would Jesus do? He would listen to us, and he

would love us, and when he disagreed with us, it would always and only be out of compassion, never oppression. There is no hurting person he would mock, or shun, or insult, or sneer at. He is so determined to pursue what is best for all of us that he died—excluded, mocked and rejected—to secure it.

If this isn't the Jesus you have heard of, then I'm sorry. It is the Jesus who I seek to live with and for. And it is the Jesus whose words you'll hear in this book as we take a careful look at what the Bible really says about gender identity, and what that means for people who experience uncertainty or struggles with their gender identity; for those who love those who experience those struggles; and for churches who are (or should be) seeking to support those who experience gender-identity conflicts.

WHY THIS BOOK?

I'm writing this book because there's a revolution happening in Western culture that is exploding our assumptions and traditions of what it means to be a man or a woman.

This revolution is flipping over the tables of centuries-old norms. And there's some good that can come from it. It is good, for example, that people who experience distress about their gender identity are able to talk more openly and honestly about their struggles and feelings without everyone in society thinking they are a freak. Society is now attempting to help people who experience doubts and struggles with their gender identity, rather than push those people to the margins.

With that revolution comes a debate—a debate about what it means, if anything, to be a man or a woman. In this debate, there are many voices. Some are loud; many are quiet. Some are unfair and strident, from a variety of perspectives. Others are measured and kind, from a variety of positions. Some are well-represented in the media, and others struggle to be heard.

I think it's important that God's voice is heard in this debate. That's what this book is about. It is not a medical or psychological study, nor is it a statistical analysis or political manifesto. It's aiming, as clearly as possible, to let God's voice be heard.

This is a book for busy, thoughtful people who want to consider what the Bible says about transgenderism, how that applies to situations they'll likely face, and, possibly, what that means for the struggles they or their loved ones are experiencing now. I'm writing for you if you want to learn more, love better, and are open to considering what God has to say about sex and gender in his word.

The only assumption taken in this book, and an assumption I'd ask you to be open to if you do not already subscribe to it, is that the Bible is God's word. Maybe you accept that truth; maybe you do not. But it is worth taking a look at every available resource to see what guidance it has for such a difficult, painful, emotive issue. And so the only favor I ask is that you read this book right through and see it as a whole. This is a hard issue, and it is not a simple one. Each chapter is, in many ways, reliant on other chapters, and no one chapter says everything that I think needs to be said.

Here's where we're heading. We'll begin with three short introductory chapters, to gain a grasp of how we've gotten to where we are as a culture, what it means to be transgender, and why and how people reach such different positions in this debate.

In chapters 5 to 7, we will examine what the Bible says about humanity, and therefore about gender.

Chapters 8 to 11 ground that in the real lives of ordinary people:

- what this means for those who wish to love transgender neighbors
- what Jesus says to those who experience gender dysphoria or who identify as transgender
- how Jesus challenges local churches to show compassion to every person that enters our churches, regardless of who they are and what they think, while also taking seriously the truth of God's word
- how parents might speak to their children about gender identity.

At the end, there is a chapter of answers to important questions that the previous chapters haven't dealt with.

There's one more reason I've written this book: I'd love for the church not to be constantly playing catch-up in the culture. We shouldn't let it always be the case that the church addresses an issue only when the broader culture takes it up first. Christians lagged behind, for example, in showing a compassionate grace-and-truth response to homosexuality. Some of us forgot about truth. Most of us forgot about grace.

I pray that this won't happen again when it comes to gender identity. When it comes to speaking truth, showing compassion, and seeking justice, the church should be leading, not following. I hope this book is a contribution to that cause.

This book is not the last word on the subject or the last word in this debate. It won't satisfy every objection or answer every question. It's a start, not a finish.

In Matthew's Gospel we read of Jesus that...

> *When he saw the crowds, he had compassion for them,*
> *because they were harassed and helpless, like sheep without*
> *a shepherd. (9 v 36)*

Using Jesus as my example and my guide, I hope to offer in this book a compassionate way forward; a way that is different and, I believe, offers greater hope than many of the other voices in this debate. I hope it is helpful to you, even as and when it is provocative. My greatest prayer above all is that, if and when what you read is hard to hear, you will remember that the God who speaks to you in the Bible is the same God who loves you so much that he came, lived, and even died to strengthen bruised reeds and fan flickering flames.

2. HOW WE GOT TO WHERE WE ARE

You might remember the moment you first heard that Bruce Jenner didn't want to be Bruce anymore.

It was 2015 when Jenner—an Olympic champion, American hero, and step-father to the famous Kardashians—was interviewed by the journalist Diane Sawyer about his experience as a man who had long lived with a deep secret. All his life, though revered as a model of athleticism and masculinity, Bruce Jenner believed he was really a woman. He defined himself as being transgender.

If you've seen the interview, you see someone deeply hurt, wounded, and unable to find peace—someone still seeking self-acceptance despite possessing wealth and celebrity. Grieving for someone I had never met, my insides hurt as I watched the pained interview where Jenner laid bare his soul.

Fast-forward to a few months later and Bruce Jenner made a surprise appearance on the front cover of *Vanity Fair* magazine. Wearing lingerie and posing provocatively on a barstool, hands tucked behind back, Jenner copied the hyper-femininity and exaggerated sex appeal that we're used to seeing on the covers of magazines at the checkout in a grocery store. The cover was an act of self-revelation, for Jenner's appearance signaled a transition to fully identifying as and living as a woman. "Call Me Caitlyn," the cover proclaimed. The picture is now world famous.

A super-celebrity and cultural icon, Caitlyn Jenner, was born. The message to the world was clear: men can become women if they feel or perceive themselves to be women, and vice versa.

The media could not get enough of Jenner's transformation. News quickly came that Jenner would star in a reality-TV show, documenting the historic transformation. Jenner's new twitter account under this identity broke records in how quickly it gained millions of new followers.

It seems that this question of being "transgender" has catapulted to the front of culture at a dizzyingly fast pace. Transgender had been a topic that barely registered on most people's radars. Now, and quite suddenly, gender identity became the most fashionable social-justice issue of our day.

QUESTIONS NEEDING ANSWERS

2015 seems like a long time ago now. Today, Facebook offers over fifty gender options to its members. Debates about restroom usage overwhelm social media. States like New York are fining citizens who fail to use the preferred pronoun of transgender citizens.[1]

And it is all happening fast—so fast that it is hard to catch up, let alone understand the debate, how we got here, and what we would like to say. But all of us need an answer to questions such as:

- Can a man become a woman? Can a woman become a man?

---

[1] See www.washingtonpost.com/news/volokh-conspiracy/wp/2016/05/17/you-can-be-fined-for-not-calling-people-ze-or-hir-if-thats-the-pronoun-they-demand-that-you-use/?utm_term=.3928798cd12d

- How and when should children be confronted with the debates about gender?
- What are we to do with children who are a member of one biological sex but feel as though they were born in the wrong body?
- What do we say to someone experiencing these feelings and desires?
- How do we love and help those who are deeply hurting?

These questions go deeper than simply what we understand by "gender." They go to what we understand by "humanity": who we are, how we got here, what it means to be a human, and what role (if any) God plays in that. Beneath the news stories, and beneath the questions that many are wrestling with personally, are the questions of what story we will live by; how we will make sense of our lives, and what will give us our identity and our confidence.

We will get to all that later in this book. But first we need to ask: how did we get here? The temptation in answering that question is to give one simple answer. But there aren't simple answers. Lots of factors have brought us to where we are today. Many streams flow into the transgender debate.

RELATIVISM

Relativism is the approach to truth that all of us in the global West are swimming in, perhaps without realizing it. Relativism says that meaning and truth are relative, so that what is right for one person may be wrong for another person. You might have heard someone else say, or heard yourself think, "You can't tell me what to do," or, "There's no such thing as absolute truth," or, "That's great for you, but it's not for me." Those sayings are examples of how relativism influences our thinking today.

Relativism denies that there's any one "right" way to understand the world. There are only stories, not a grand Story. So there's Islam, Christianity, and Judaism, and lots and lots of other religions, and none are true in all times and all places and for all people. A religion is but one example of how someone could choose to live his or her life, but it isn't authoritative for everyone. Any attempt to claim that it is is just a ruse to gain power over someone else.

POST-CHRISTENDOM

By almost all accounts and statistics, Christianity is in decline in the West. It's hard to measure decline, but for the most part, Christianity's cultural influence is dying. This means that the moral truths that Christianity teaches are having less and less impact with each passing year and generation. Fewer people are attending church, which means that the devotion people once gave to Christianity seems to be receding. A growing biblical illiteracy means that individuals are growing more and more unfamiliar with the biblical narrative and the categories of the Bible that so many in the West simply took for granted. With declining influence, greater opportunity emerges for different value or ethical systems to displace Christian morality as the widely accepted norm.

What you make of this rapid change depends on what you think of Christianity. But no one disputes that this change is felt especially in matters related to sexual ethics. Over the last generation, there has been growing acceptance of gay and lesbian relationships, declining marriage rates and rising divorce rates, and more people living together before (or instead of) marrying. All of these social changes can only take place in a context where Christian ways of understanding the world are seen as optional, irrelevant, or (as is increasingly the case) hateful and bigoted.

It is impossible for any society to not have some form of morality; so the question is: whose morality is going to reign supreme? The passing of one moral framework means that another one must take its place, and all evidence suggests that a secular framework is the likely candidate. As Christian morality was guarded and taught in a Christianized society, the same is equally true of a secular framework in a secular society—which makes it likely that biblical Christians will be on the wrong side of a secular culture.

Where you live may not seem post-Christian. America, for instance, has large numbers of Christians. But the most influential sectors of US culture—academia, media, entertainment, art, law—are increasingly no longer influenced by Christianity, because those who occupy places of prestige, influence, and cultural impact are in most cases not Christians, nor are they sympathetic to Christian views.

RADICAL INDIVIDUALISM

Individualism says everyone gets to write their own script. In many ways, this follows downstream from relativism. What an individual wills or wants is the highest good, and it is wrong to tell someone that his or her choices or beliefs are wrong or immoral. An emphasis on the individual bearing individual rights has given rise to an understanding of the individual that is "liberated" from all forms of other duties. The greatest sin—in fact, the only sin—is judging someone else.

Long ago (and still today in many parts of the world), societies did not think in terms of individuals or individual rights. Instead, a focus on families, clans, and community was the dominant way that each person understood their existence. In such a society the question is not, "What is best for me?" or, "What makes me happy?" but, "What is best for my tribe?" and, "What makes my tribe most secure or honored?"

If this approach seems outdated or unimaginable to us, it shows how "Western" we are, without realizing it! If it seems unfair and restrictive, it shows how judgmental "non-judgmental" people can be!

Of course, not all forms of individualism are bad. An emphasis on individualism can and often does prioritize the dignity of each person. The fact that governments believe that citizens have rights that are inviolable is a good example of how individualism has been of great benefit. Radical individualism rests on this idea—but then it goes far further than that.

SEXUAL REVOLUTION

The sexual revolution of the 1960s gave rise to the popular idea that "if it feels good, do it." There's arguably no greater stream feeding our current climate than the sexual revolution's revolt against what it considered "puritan" or "prudish" sexuality. The upheaval of the sexual revolution taught that our bodies are our own, and for us to enjoy in whatever way we want.

If you want evidence of how the sexual revolution has impacted the world, look at the entertainment industry. In every corner of it, there is an unchallenged (and unchallengeable) assumption that sexual freedom is the highest standard for personal fulfillment.

This period when Christian ideas of sexual morality were challenged and overturned coincided with (and very possibly contributed to) industrialized hormonal contraception. This is not the book to debate the pros

and cons of the pill—but one consequence of its avail-
ability was to sever the connection between sex and pro-
creation. This was nothing short of revolutionary. While
people in times past engaged in pre-marital sex, there was
always the potential for a pregnancy to occur. Not any
more—and this has enormous repercussions for how society thinks about the purpose of sex. No longer is sex
assumed to take place only in marriage. The idea that sex
outside marriage is wrong has been overturned, and the
risk associated with sex outside marriage has been negat-
ed. The legalization of abortion in 1973 (in the US) and
the resultant lack of stigma completed the separation of
having sex and giving birth.

The sexual revolution resulted in positive developments
for women's rights. It also led to declining marriage rates
and an explosion in the divorce rate. At least for the first
couple decades, it resulted in an increase in the number
of abortions being performed each year. We in the global
West are living downstream from the powerful waves of
the sexual revolution.

GNOSTICISM

Gnosticism is an ancient view of ourselves that is in fashion again today. In ancient times (it both predated Christianity and permeated much of the early church) it taught
that the physical world—"matter"—is bad and broken,
and that what really matters is for a person to seek spiritual escape away from the world. Gnosticism emphasizes
that a person's self-awareness is different than and more
important than their physical body.

Gnosticism says that there is an inherent tension between our true selves and the bodies we inhabit. The idea
that our true self is different than the body we live in

communicates that our body is something less than us, and can be used, shaped, and changed to match how we feel.

The concept that our gender can be different than our biological sex is a modern form of the old Gnostic idea. What this means, practically, is that a man can identify as a woman, even if they have male chromosomes and the body of a man.

These are the streams that flow into our society, and explain why the transgender debate has not just come to the forefront of our cultural consciousness, but why it has moved on so rapidly. It did not come out of nowhere. It came from a confluence of these powerful, though often unnoticed and unchallenged, cultural influences.

And all this means that there are two unforgivable sins in a postmodern, post-Christianized, individualist world. The first is to judge someone else. The second is to fail to fulfill your desires.

DO GOOD

Two millennia ago, the apostle Paul wrote to a group of Christians:

> *Let us not grow weary of doing good, for in due season we will reap, if we do not give up. (Galatians 6 v 9)*

Christians are called to do good. That much is simple. But what is good? That is more complex. For some, "doing good" means going wherever the culture goes; and sometimes they are right. For others, "doing good" means rejecting wherever culture is going and calling "bad" whatever culture says is "good." Sometimes they are right. All of us, depending on our characters, will tend instinctively to accept or reject cultural shifts, and label our predispositions "good."

But the Christian view of "good" is not defined simply by agreeing or disagreeing with the cultural moment God has decided to place us in. And so it is often complex and quite tiring to work out what "good" is—let alone to then live it out, regardless of whether that puts us in favor with society or at odds with society. When we grow weary, we tend to do what we find easier—either pulling up the drawbridge or just going with the flow. But Christians are not called to do what is easier, but to do what is good. The central question here is how to think and speak and do "good" when it comes to the transgender debate—and to the real people, and real pain, that are part of that debate.

3. THE LANGUAGE

What do we actually mean when we say "transgender"?

To define that term, we need to take a look at other new words that have been developed to explain the growing number of sexual and gender identities that are part of the gender-identity revolution. There are five terms that we all need a working definition of:

- sex
- gender
- gender identity
- gender dysphoria
- transgender.

IT'S A BOY, IT'S A GIRL

Every era and every society has its own ways of announcing impending births. In ours, there are wonderfully imaginative surprises—one of my favorites is the parents giving each of their moms a t-shirt that says, "World's Best Grandma." Sometimes on Facebook I see a man and woman in the background holding hands with a little sign saying "Coming soon...," or an older sibling holding a picture of an ultrasound scan with the photo entitled, "I'm a big brother/sister" (delete as applicable!).

In the US, the latest phenomenon is "gender-reveal parties." A couple will have a party at their home and invite friends over, and the couple will have come up with a clever way to reveal not just that they are expecting, but also whether the baby is a boy or girl. One way I heard of is for the couple simultaneously to bite into a cupcake where the cake mix is made blue or pink with food coloring, so that the moment the inside of the cupcake is revealed to the crowd, whether the baby is a boy or a girl is also announced.

Gender-reveal parties reflect a view that has been universally accepted up until very recently: gender is connected to sex. The announcement of the gender at the party is based on the assumption that the gender of the baby will follow the sex that was revealed on the ultrasound scan. It is ironic that gender-reveal parties have exploded in popularity at the same time as the idea that sex and gender can be uncoupled altogether.

"Gender" is not a new word. But gender does not mean what it used to.

SEX, GENDER, AND GENDER IDENTITY

There are several ways to think about a person's sex. Sex can refer to biological make-up or composition. Men have XY chromosomes. Women have XX chromosomes. There are hormonal and reproductive differences between men and women that result from chromosomal difference. From our bodies down to our cells, the biological sex of those born men and those born women are different.

Then there are our "primary sex characteristics," which refer to the differences in reproductive systems. "Secondary sex characteristics" refer to the other general physical differences between adult men and women. Men, for example, tend to have broader shoulders and be taller than women. Women tend to have wider hips and be shorter.

According to the American Psychological Association, "gender" refers to the...

> *"... attitudes, feelings, and behaviors that a given culture associates with a person's biological sex. Behavior that is compatible with cultural expectations is referred to as gender-normative; behaviors that are viewed as incompatible with these expectations constitute gender non-conformity."* [2]

In traditional societies—that includes virtually every society until the last decade or so in parts of the West—gender has been attached to sex. It's the culturally appropriate expression of your sex. So if your sex is "female," your gender is "female."

The way we express our gender varies from culture to culture. There is no one way or right way to express gender—each culture has its own gender norms. Think about *Braveheart*, one of my all-time favorite movies. In *Braveheart*, the 13th-century Scottish warrior William Wallace wore a kilt—because in Scotland men wore kilts (and often still do today, at ceremonial events such as weddings). In other contexts—21st-century America, for instance—a kilt looks like a woman's skirt. It would be odd, therefore, for William Wallace to show up in Nashville, Tennessee (quite apart from the fact that there was no Nashville in the 13th century), wearing an item of clothing that is associated in that time and place with feminine dress attire. In Scotland, however, it is perfectly masculine for men to wear kilts because that is associated with manhood. There's nothing about the item of clothing itself

---

2 www.apa.org/pi/lgbt/resources/sexuality-definitions.pdf.

that makes it masculine or feminine. It is what a culture assigns to the object that makes it masculine or feminine, or either.

Gender has always been expressed in different ways. What has changed today is that many now see gender as unattached to sex. That is, you don't just express gender differently; you can be a different gender. Your sex may be "female," but that does not necessarily mean that you—as regards your gender—are "female."

Because of advances in medical science, we are the first generation that are able to seek to make sex follow gender, rather than the other way around. There are now medical procedures that allow people whose sex is male and who identify their gender as female to have their bodies surgically reshaped to reflect that female gender.

That leads us to a new term: "gender identity." Gender identity is a person's self-perception of whether they are male or female, masculine or feminine.[3]

All of us have a "gender identity." Some people feel their gender identity does not align with their biological sex. When someone experiences distress, inner anguish, or discomfort from sensing a conflict between their gender identity and their biological sex, that person is experiencing gender dysphoria—a mismatch between the gender that matches their biological sex and the gender that they feel themselves to be.[4] It is crucial to understand that this is a genuine experience. People with gender dysphoria experience the feeling that their biological body is lying. A person in this situation really thinks that he or she is, should be, or would feel better as, the gender that is opposite to their biological sex, or no gender at all.

---

3 For more on this, see Mark Yarhouse, *Understanding Gender Dysphoria: Navigating Transgender Issues in a Changing Culture* (IVP USA, 2015), page 17.

4 Yarhouse, *Understanding Gender Dysphoria,* page 19.

GENDER DYSPHORIA AND TRANSGENDER

People who experience distress, anguish, and conflict from their perceived gender identity are not perverts or freaks. It is an unchosen experience—it is never something that someone should just "get over." And no two experiences of gender dysphoria are completely alike. Research based on listening to those who are "gender dysphoric" indicates that there are degrees of dysphoria, ranging along a spectrum from "mild" to "severe." People who identify as transgender report disproportionately higher rates of mental-health problems than the rest of the general population, including depression, suicide, and thoughts of suicide.[5]

Most important to remember is that these are real people. They are sons and daughters, brothers and sisters. They are people who may have been sitting in the pew behind us for two decades, or who work at the desk next to us Monday to Friday, or who are part of our families. They may, of course, be you. And this needs constantly underlining—because when the debate begins to get heated in the language that is used, or the accusations that are thrown, or assumptions that are made, real people are getting burned.

None of this means that a person who experiences gender dysphoria necessarily identifies as "transgender." Someone may experience conflict between their gender identity and their biological sex, but not see that experience as the determining factor in how they perceive themselves. A person who experiences dysphoria may very well choose to live in alignment with their biological sex. Dysphoria is an experience; it is not necessarily a lens or "identity" through which a person views his or her life.

---

5 See Yarhouse, *Understanding Gender Dysphoria,* chapters 3-5.

But to follow that desire to some extent is to be "transgender." Transgender is an umbrella term for the state or condition of identifying or expressing a gender identity that does not match a person's genetic sex. It may mean dressing in the culturally determined dress of the gender that someone identifies with; it may involve someone having hormonal treatment to seek to bring their chemical balance into alignment with that gender; and it could include undergoing surgical treatment to alter their bodies. It may also mean not identifying as one gender all the time (which is often termed "gender fluid") or not identifying as male or female at all (usually called "non-binary" or "agender").

TWO QUICK QUESTIONS

Does anything "cause" gender dysphoria? This is a question for which there is no definitive answer. This is an important point, because many people who take a variety of views in the transgender "debate" do so by making bold claims without actual evidence to back those claims up. That's very unhelpful, whether the claims are offered in support of a fluid view of gender, or in support of a more traditional approach. The best research has offered no conclusive evidence that experiences of gender dysphoria are the result of any particular factor or factors.[6]

How common is transgenderism? Though exact numbers are difficult to nail down, the Williams Institute at the University of California estimates that 0.3% of the US population—

---

6 For a helpful overview of the dominant theories for what causes experiences of gender dysphoria, see chapter three of Yarhouse, *Understanding Gender Dysphoria*. See also Lawrence S. Mayer and Paul R. McHugh, "Sexuality and Gender: Findings from the Biological, Psychological, and Social Sciences," in *The New Atlantis*, Number 50, Fall 2016. Available at: www.thenewatlantis.com/publications/number-50-fall-2016.

or about 700,000 people—is transgender.[7] As society becomes more socially tolerant, people reporting gender dysphoria or identifying as transgender will likely increase.

THE FIVE TERMS YOU NEED TO KNOW

The rapid dawn of transgender discussion in the mainstream of our culture has spawned a lot of new words or redefined words. But the only five terms you'll really need in this book, and that hopefully this chapter has helpfully defined, are:

- gender
- sex
- gender identity
- gender dysphoria
- transgender

If you are interested, on page 165 you'll find a helpful list of many more of the terms that you'll likely come across and what they mean, courtesy of Joe Carter, a Christian cultural commentator and a professor of journalism. But these five words or terms provide us with sufficient "language" to be able to engage with the transgender debate.

---

7 http://williamsinstitute.law.ucla.edu/wp-content/uploads/Gates-How-Many-People-LGBT-Apr-2011.pdf.

4. ON MAKING A DECISION

"**D**o you really believe what you believe is really real?" That was a question posed to me by a professor back in 2006. I was twenty at the time, I was a committed Christian, and—until he asked that—I thought I was secure in my beliefs.

But that question unsettled me. It required me to think deeply about the biggest aspects of my faith. I had to give an answer, and "The Bible tells me so" wasn't sufficient. I had to reach deeper about how I understood what authority is, how I understood what was true, and why the sources of my faith were trustworthy.

That question is a question that requires all of us to consider not just what we believe, but why we believe it.

It's a question that leads to other big questions.

- What is reality?
- What is the nature of the world around us?
- What is a human being?
- What happens to a person at death?
- Why is it possible to know anything at all?
- How do we know what is right and wrong? [8]

---

8 These questions come from James Sire's *The Universe Next Door* (IVP USA, 2004).

We all answer those questions. We may do it with a great deal of angst and heart-searching, or we may do it unconsciously without even realizing it. But we do do it.

These questions require us to evaluate our worldview. They require us to unearth our deepest convictions about the world, our purpose, and morality. One scholar defines a worldview this way:

> *"A commitment, a fundamental orientation of the heart, that can be expressed as a story or in a set of presuppositions (assumptions which may be true, partially true or entirely false) which we hold (consciously or subconsciously, consistently or inconsistently) about the basic constitution of reality, and that provides the foundation on which we live and move and have our being."* [9]

In other words, a worldview is the sum of the beliefs we hold at the deepest levels of our being—consciously or unconsciously—about where the ultimate meaning of reality is found. Every person on earth—atheist, Christian, Muslim, agnostic, Mormon, Hindu, Buddhist, everyone—has a worldview. If you're reading this right now, you don't have the luxury of not having a worldview. You have a worldview. So what is it?

HOW TO CHOOSE WHETHER TO EAT ICE CREAM

Our worldview comes to the surface whenever we need to decide how to live in some way.

How do you and I work out what is right and what is wrong in terms of our beliefs and actions, particularly when faced with big decisions that we may only get one shot at making?

---

9 James Sire, *The Universe Next Door,* page 17.

Ultimately, in finding the answer, you are looking for a source of:

- *Authority:* Who has the right to tell me what to do?
- *Knowledge:* Who knows what is best for me to do?
- *Trustworthiness:* Who loves me and wants what is best for me?

Find a person, or an institution, or a book that offers you those three and that's where you will turn to make decisions. There are lots of options for how people will answer these questions.

Many answer these questions by appealing to their family, their nation, their political associations, their religion, their friends, their feelings; or to entertainment or science. And we can find their source of authority, knowledge, and trustworthiness in different places on a case-by-case basis.

Think of everyday choices we make all the time. Let's use a familiar example (at least to me!): how do I decide whether to have ice cream?

I could choose to listen to my feelings, which are telling me it would be great to taste ice cream. Or I could look to my reason—I'm dieting and should not have any ice cream. Perhaps I will locate the basis for my decision in the way my mom brought me up—I will pass on the ice cream because my mom warned me against eating too much sugar. Or I could be fasting from ice cream, because of my choice to submit my decision to a particular religious code.

So in that decision-making progress, there are a host of different sources of authority that I could choose to "listen to" in reaching my decision on whether to have ice cream: feelings, reason, family, religion. And this is just on a simple matter like whether to eat ice cream! (We haven't even got to choosing which flavor to pick, an equally difficult decision!)

Now, why does any of this matter around debates of sexuality and gender?

As I mentioned in chapter two, the West is undergoing a profound transformation as the era of post-Christendom is ushered in. We have a great range of options among which to find our source of authority, knowledge, and trustworthiness.

If we differ in our answer to the source of authority, knowledge, and trust in our decision-making, we shouldn't be surprised if we're miles apart once we each reach our destination—our decision on a particular issue or action. When it comes to the question of how we should think about gender, and transgenderism, there are very different answers. They can be miles apart, and often people cannot understand why others stand in such a different place than they do in this debate. It helps to remember that the journey to those different answers started with this question of how to decide how to live. That is where the fork in the road comes. In a sense, as we think about our views on an issue like gender and transgenderism (the "destination"), we need to begin at the start of the journey and assess why we think the way we do and therefore make the decisions we do.

THE SEARCH FOR AN AUTHORITY WE CAN TRUST

Especially since World War II, but even from as far back as the 16th century, there has been a crisis of authority in the Western world.

Child sex-abuse scandals, and before that the way that professing Christians practiced and justified race-based slavery, made it reasonable to question whether churches could be trusted.

Political scandals like Watergate and senior politicians' sexual affairs (and their cover-ups) lowered the respect we have for our leaders.

Videos of police officers beating and shooting unarmed African Americans eroded trust in civil authority.

The unraveling of political ideologies once popular in the 20th century—most obviously fascism and then communism—have made us wary of allowing political systems to direct our personal decisions.

It has proven possible to use science in good ways and bad. And however many scientific advances our race makes, science can't provide "ought to" explanations for who I should choose to marry, and then whether I should leave my wife a few years later.

In this age, when claims to authority are challenged and contested, where is left for us to look for a source of authority, knowledge and trustworthiness?

Me. My self.

It seems so obvious. After all, who has more right to tell me how to live than me? Who knows me better than me? Who can I trust to want what's best for me more than me?

Post-modern individualism agrees with this. The sexual revolution tells me that the highest goal is self-fulfillment, achieved through following my feelings; and relativism makes it possible for me to pursue these goals without anyone being allowed to say, "No, that's wrong."

So we decide according to our reason or (more normally) our feelings, or both. Think about how often you hear others say of a decision or an opinion (and maybe you catch yourself saying this too), "I feel like…" or "I think that…" It's so much part of the prevailing wind of our culture that we hardly notice it. It's obvious, it's natural, it's right—right?

THINKING ABOUT *ME*

Dig a little deeper though, and the idea of looking to our feelings or reason—to our selves—to make decisions and decide what is right starts to unravel. First, we all live in community. Every decision affects those around us, often in ways we cannot predict or do not see. How do I know my decision will have no adverse effects on anyone's life and fulfillment, at any point? That would require perfect knowledge. None of us are that clever! And none of us have the authority or right to do something that will affect someone else adversely—including in ways that we cannot see.

Second, do I really know myself that well? I have never lived before. I may identify a problem with my fulfillment, but I cannot know I have rightly identified the solution. I don't know how I will feel, who I will be, or what I will need tomorrow or next year, let alone in a decade. If I had acted on every feeling or thought that looked good to me when I was 18, my life would be very different, and much worse!

Third, and perhaps most surprisingly, I have to ask myself, "Am I really to be trusted to want what's best for me?" We've all acted on our feelings in a way that we later regretted (to take some everyday examples, speaking unkindly to a loved one, or failing to study for an exam). We can all, when we think about it, point to moments when we did something that not only did not improve or fulfill us, but actually did the reverse. We've all reasoned something out, acted on that logic, and then found that what seemed so reasonable wasn't.

So, it turns out the self is not such a good place to look to for authority, knowledge, and trustworthiness.

But... where else is there to go? The self may have its limitations, but we have to make decisions somehow; we have to view the world in some way—and the self still seems a better bet than religious institutions, secular organizations, or previous generations.

A BETTER STORY, A GREATER SOURCE

The Bible tells of a different story, for it gives a different script on which to understand where to look for perfect authority, perfect knowledge, and perfect trustworthiness.

The very first line of the Bible is familiar to most, but no less fundamental for that:

> *In the beginning, God created the heavens and the earth.*
>
> *(Genesis 1 v 1)*

This world has a Creator. And what is made belongs to its maker; so the Creator has authority. What is made is best known by its maker; the Creator has knowledge.

Since I am part of the creation, and alive within creation, God has the right to tell me what to do. And he has the knowledge necessary always to understand what I should do—what is best for me and the world. There is a Creator, and he is all powerful, all-knowing, and all-wise.

But that does not mean that he is good. Why should you and I trust our Creator to tell us what really is best for us? Because of what he has done for his world:

> *God so loved the world, that he gave his only Son, that whoever believes in him should not perish but have eternal life. (John 3 v 16)*

There is a Creator who can be trusted to want what's truly best for you. He wants your best so much that he came in the person of his Son and died for you. The Bible tells us of a crucified Creator. God loves you much more than you love you.

So passages such as Proverbs 3 v 5-6 are not only commands, but promises...

> *Trust in the* LORD *with all your heart, and do not lean on your own understanding. In all your ways acknowledge him, and he will make straight your paths.*

A crucified Creator is a God who has the authority to tell us what to do, who has the wisdom to know what is best for us, and who has proved that he can be trusted to tell us what is best for us.

And so the Bible reveals to us a God who has the authority to demand your obedience, and who has the character that deserves your respect. This God really does know what's best for me and he really does want what's best for me.

A LAW THAT BRINGS FREEDOM

When the God who has authority, and knowledge, and trustworthiness tells us to do something, that something is actually what brings us liberty, because its source is the crucified Creator who has proven that he knows and wants what is best for us:

> *But the one who looks into the perfect law, the law of liberty, and perseveres, being no hearer who forgets but a doer who acts, he will be blessed in his doing. (James 1 v 25)*

So when we say to ourselves, or to others, "You should obey God," what we mean is, *We want what God deserves (your obedience) and we want what is best for you (your obedience)*.

This is why Christians hold views or believe things that go against what may come to us naturally or instinctively. Christians have found a better source for authority, knowledge, and trust than our own reason or feelings—or our own traditions or assumptions. "Because that's the way I've always thought" or, "That's the way we've always thought" or, "It's just wrong, isn't it?" are no better answers than, "Because that's the way I feel," or, "How can something that feels so right be wrong?"

It's crucial—especially when self and Scripture disagree—to know why we are thinking and deciding what we are deciding; or, to put it a different way, it's crucial to know what our source of authority, knowledge, and trust is for that decision or opinion. This holds for all issues, particularly those that are most controversial—including issues of sexual morality and the debate about transgender identity.

After all, when all of the noise is stripped away, what is driving our culture's ideas about sexuality and gender? Fundamentally, the biggest issue that drives a wedge between an increasingly secularized culture and the Christian worldview is the question of where we locate authority, knowledge, and trustworthiness. Who has authority to tell me how to live, to decide what is right or wrong? Who knows what is best? Who can I trust to lead me to what will fulfill me? Our various answers to those questions will set us on routes that lead to very, very different places.

The Christian answer is to locate authority, knowledge, and trust where it can find a firm, stable, fulfilling foundation—in the crucified Creator. He may not always agree with our feelings or our reason—but he can be trusted, and he knows what he's talking about, and he has the right to tell us how to live. His words are good to listen to and to obey. And, over the next three chapters, this is what we will be doing.

5. WELL-DESIGNED

Imagine yourself on a tour of an airplane-manufacturing plant. You are there to see a new, cutting-edge model. As you begin your tour, you talk with engineers about the overall design. They talk about the plane's speed, its power, and its seating capacity.

Next, you head out onto the floor of the plant where hundreds of workers each have a unique task. You stroll past each station. Workers are assembling the engine. There's a station for wiring all the cockpit instrumentation. Further down the factory floor, you see workers putting upholstery on seats that will go inside the plane. Each is working from a plan—the blueprint for the plane.

Then, at the very end of this enormous facility, you see it: the plane itself. It is still in an almost skeletal form. But a design is taking shape that will make an insanely heavy object fly at amazing speeds—and if any of these workers fail to meet expectations, something could go wrong with the plane. A mistake in constructing the engine, or a failure to tighten the propeller components properly, will lead to catastrophe.

Every part of the plane's design is intentional. Nothing here happens by accident or guesswork. Each part of the plane is relying on other parts of the plane to do their job so it can do its job. The parts are interlinked and dependent.

GOD'S BLUEPRINT

When we look at the Bible, we see a similar story take shape as we read how God created the world. There was a Designer, and he had a plan for how he was going to make the world. There was a blueprint that God had in mind. And, once he had built his creation, he stood back (as it were) and nodded:

> *And God saw everything that he had made, and behold, it was very good. And there was evening and there was morning, the sixth day. (Genesis 1 v 31)*

God's creation was "very good." It was not average and it was not purposeless. God's act of creating was successful in every part, and it was intentional in every part. Genesis 1 – 2 shows us that the God of the Bible does not create by chaos but according to a purpose. And his purpose is brilliant—whether it is trees, or mountains, or stars or atoms or babies' fingers, creation is full of awe-inspiring sights, sounds and smells.

And God's creative brilliance climaxes with humanity:

> *Then God said, "Let us make man in our image, after our likeness. And let them have dominion over the fish of the sea and over the birds of the heavens and over the livestock and over all the earth and over every creeping thing that creeps on the earth."*
> *So God created man in his own image,*
> *in the image of God he created him;*
> *male and female he created them.*
> *And God blessed them. And God said to them, "Be fruitful and multiply and fill the earth and subdue it, and have dominion over the fish of the sea and over the birds of the heavens and over every living thing that moves on*

the earth." And God said, "Behold, I have given you every
plant yielding seed that is on the face of all the earth, and
every tree with seed in its fruit. You shall have them for
food." (Genesis 1 v 26-29)

The highpoint of the story of creation is God's act of
making mankind. Genesis paints a picture of a God who,
like an artist, finishes a masterpiece with extra care, attention, and precision.

Humanity is the highpoint because there is something
unique about mankind: only humans bear God's image.

"The image of God" is a somewhat mysterious category that theologians have debated for centuries. All agree,
though, that to bear God's image means that there's a spe-
cial relationship that only humans have with God. According to one, Wayne Grudem:

> *"The fact that man is in the image of God means that man*
> *is like and represents God."* [10]

Humans are not identical to God, but they are made to be
like God in features such as their moral aspects, spiritual aspects, mental aspects, and relational aspects. Humans
can know God in ways that the rest of creation cannot.
Rabbits do not debate among themselves the existence
and nature of the divine while nibbling grass, and fish do
not consider the moral complexities of their lives while
swimming around. Humans do consider these things and
debate these questions. Further, humans were assigned the
task to "subdue" creation—to rule over it on God's behalf.

We are made to represent God, to relate to God, and
to rule on behalf of God. It is from being made in God's

---

10 *Systematic Theology: An Introduction to Christian Doctrine* (Zondervan, 1994), page
442.

image that humans possess inherent dignity. Quoting Grudem again:

> *"We are the culmination of God's infinitely wise and skillful work of creation."*

No one—not the state, not any philosophy, not any social movement—can give humanity more dignity and worth than God can. Our value and worth does not come from ourselves; it is God-given.

MORE THAN THE SUM OF YOUR PARTS

Come back to the aircraft hanger. How much is the engine worth? If you add up the value of all its parts you will get one answer. But if you consider that all the parts together have made an engine, you will get a bigger number. The engine has greater value than the sum of its constituent parts, because it has been made intentionally, as an engine, and as a crucial part of a greater plan. So you and I are of more worth than our parts add up to, or than your contribution to your nation's economy (otherwise the unemployed would be worthless), or to our species' future (otherwise those without children would be of less value). You have been made intentionally, as an image-bearing human, as a crucial part of God's greater creative plan.

And every aspect of who we are carries and reflects that dignity—our minds, our hearts, and our bodies. All are created, and all therefore carry value and are designed to have dignity.

This means matter matters. Our bodies matter. Your body is not arbitrary; it is intentional. While you are more than your body, you are not less. We are not just a collection of atoms and synapses that happen to be conscious.

Nor are we God-aware souls trapped in the materials of this universe. We are living, feeling, emotional, embodied beings, designed to relate to and reflect the Creator with each part of ourselves.

GOD'S RIGHT TO SPEAK

The earth is the LORD'*s and the fullness thereof, the world and those who dwell therein, for he has founded it upon the seas and established it upon the rivers. (Psalm 24 v 1-2)*

In other words, because God made this world, this world belongs to God. We are a part of God's creation; we are creatures with a Creator. The best way to live is according to the blueprint that God designed; and by playing the part that God designed humanity to perform. As creatures, we can't rewrite the blueprint of our design out of our own will. A plane's engine cannot decide to be a wheel, because the wheel is defined with a different purpose in mind. We have neither the authority nor the ability to rewrite or reconfigure how God made his world. It's his creation; we're just living in it. And, since our bodies are part of his world, made by him, his authority extends to us. This is his creation, and we are his creation.

So this is why, ultimately, God has authority in the transgender debate. His voice deserves to be heard, and his opinion needs to carry ultimate weight. This isn't a debate between "cisgender" [11] and "transgender" individuals, or between those who are religious and those who are secular, or between left and right. This isn't a question of whether Andrew Walker has any right to speak into this debate. This is a question of whether a Creator has the right to

---

11 See page 166 for a definition of "cisgender."

speak about his creation. And it is a question of whether a Creator has more knowledge of his creation than a small part of that creation.

This is a debate on competing authorities: ourselves or God, creatures or Creator. That's what each of us has to decide; and it is a safer bet to cast your lot with the story of the Creator, who speaks authoritatively about how he made creation and why he made creation.

GOD'S CREATION HAS PURPOSE

Remember that when God finished his act of creating, he called all that he had created "very good." This is important when we think about sex and gender because when God declared his creation good, he was declaring that what he has made has purpose behind it.

The beginning of God's word makes two ideas very clear. First, God is the Creator. Second, we are creatures. These two short sentences may be the most significant of this book. Being creatures means that we aren't sovereign. Only God is sovereign. The God who creates is the God who assigns to humans what humans are, what humans are supposed to do, and how humans are to do it. Being creatures means that our highest calling and greatest pleasure is found in living in line with how God designed us. That is not to say that how God designed us is the easiest or most popular way to live. Being creatures means that we cannot re-create ourselves in any fashion or form that we desire by a simple act of the will or the complex work of a surgeon. When we as creatures reject the Creator's blueprint, we are both rebelling against the natural order of how things objectively are, and (though it may not seem like it) we are rejecting the life that is going to be the highest good for us.

MORE THAN "MANKIND"

This may sound obvious, but God's blueprint included making humanity in two halves:

> *The LORD God caused a deep sleep to fall upon the man, and while he slept took one of his ribs and closed up its place with flesh. And the rib that the LORD God had taken from the man he made into a woman and brought her to the man. Then the man said,*
> *"This at last is bone of my bones*
> *and flesh of my flesh;*
> *she shall be called Woman,*
> *because she was taken out of Man."*
> *Therefore a man shall leave his father and his mother and hold fast to his wife, and they shall become one flesh.*
>
> (Genesis 2 v 21-24)

Maleness and femaleness, according to the Bible, aren't artificial categories. The differences between men and women reflect the creative intention of being made in God's image. To quote the pastor Kevin DeYoung:

> *"Far from being a mere cultural construct, God depicts the existence of a man and a woman as essential to his creational plan. The two are neither identical nor interchangeable. But when the woman, who was taken out of man, joins again with the man in sexual union, the two become one flesh (Genesis 2 v 23-24). Dividing the human race into two genders, male and female—one or the other, not both, and not one then the other—is not the invention of Victorian prudes or patriarchal oafs. It was God's idea."* [12]

---

12 "What Does the Bible Say About Transgenderism?" The Gospel Coalition, September 8, 2016, https://blogs.thegospelcoalition.org/ kevindeyoung/2016/09/08/what-does-the-bible-say-about-transgenderism.

God designed humanity in male and female forms. He chose to create two halves—not thirds, eighths, or in one single type.

What is a man? Genesis tells us that a man is a human who can be united to a woman, a wife, with whom he can physically become "one flesh" (2 v 24). A person with male anatomy is reflecting physically the fact that they are created a man. A person with female anatomy is reflecting that she is a woman. Maleness isn't only anatomy, but anatomy shows that there is maleness. And femaleness isn't only anatomy, but anatomy shows that there is femaleness. Men and women are more than just their anatomy, but they are not less.

Our anatomy tells us what gender we are. Our bodies do not lie to us.[13]

These absolute differences in men and women (chromosomes, anatomy) are accompanied by general differences in the relative strengths of being a man or woman. The broad shoulders of men aren't accidental features, but evidence of the natural strength that males were created to innately possess. The wider hips that women possess for childbearing speak to the creational design that God wove into femaleness. The protective instinct that men are often able to harness at a moment's notice isn't an evolutionary characteristic passed down from marauding cavemen— it issues from the way that God made men. Much in the same way, women tend to enjoy what we sometimes call "motherly" instincts, such as nurturing.

To misunderstand, blur, or reject the Creator's categories for humanity doesn't just put us in rebellion against the Creator and creation—it puts us at odds with how each of us was made. Since God made a "very good" world, with

13 At this point, the question of intersex people is often raised. You'll find an answer to this question on page 157.

no flaws, and since that world included humans created as men and humans created as women, to strive to become different than or even the opposite of how God made us can never result in happiness, flourishing, and joy, whatever it promises.

HOW THE CHURCH CAN GO TOO FAR

The church has often gotten gender wrong, just as society has. Unhelpful stereotypes exist around gender that can confuse individuals if they do not fit that stereotype. Being a man, for example, does not entail an automatic love of football (I don't care for football at all!); and being a woman does not demand an automatic love for cooking (I know plenty of women who do not like to cook). When society attaches stereotypes to gender and sex, it can easily send the signal that anyone who fails to conform to those stereotypes is somehow failing to epitomize manhood or womanhood.

Consider a five-year-old boy who prefers playing with dolls. With a hyper-masculine view, a parent could think that their son is displaying feminine qualities and wonder whether their child is transgender. (Some parents would be fearful about this; others would be very quick to affirm it. But both are adopting a societal basis for their view of what is a "man" or a "woman"). Or consider a seven-year-old girl who would rather play football than watch Disney princess movies. With a hyper-feminine view, a parent could view their daughter as displaying masculine qualities, and may begin to wonder whether their daughter is transgender.

Perhaps this is tempting for Christians in this generation, where, for the first time in history, questions of gender identity and a celebration of those seeking to change gender have moved into the mainstream. In our quest to stay true to God's calling as men and women, it is possible to play to extreme stereotypes in such a way as to bring confusion, and wrongly to believe that the standard or epitome of masculinity is aggression, and that the standard or epitome of femininity is playing dress-up. A man who cooks or a woman who likes watching football is not blurring inappropriate gender norms; nor is that any sort of concrete evidence that a person has gender-identity issues.

Christians must never fail to obey all that God says about gender; but equally, Christians should never go beyond what he says. When we do, we obscure what God really does say, and we have no right to complain when people misunderstand what the Bible says or reject biblical teaching along with the cultural norms that we ourselves have raised to have the same authority as God's word. Put it this way: if you as a parent care as much about your son's sporting abilities as you do his sacrificial love for others, then that suggests you have a more cultural view of masculinity than you do a biblical one.

EQUAL AND DIFFERENT

Men and women are different. Our differences extend to the deepest levels of our being: chromosomes, brains, voices, body shapes, body strengths, and reproductive systems. What our bodies are designed and destined for are different. How our bodies are designed bear witness to the difference that reflects God's creative will for humanity.

Please hear me carefully: that men and women are different makes absolutely no difference to the worth, dignity, and respect each deserve. God made men and women different in function, and equal in worth. A man's calling to lead and protect is no better, no more virtuous, and no more important than a woman's design to nurture and mother. In both instances, men and women are called to joyfully submit to the unique callings that God has made for men and women.

We can sum up God's design for men and women in this way: *equal, and different; intended, not interchangeable.* For many, accepting that is not hard at all. For some, it is deeply, even exhaustingly, difficult.

But why does this difference matter? Because we were made to complement each other in order to fulfill our God-given task in his world:

> *Be fruitful and multiply and fill the earth and subdue it, and have dominion over the fish of the sea and over the birds of the heavens and over every living thing that moves on the earth. (Genesis 1 v 28)*

The mission given to humanity as a whole is to rule the world, and a crucial part of this is to "be fruitful and multiply." In this, men and women complement each other and men and women need each other. This is seen supremely in the way we reproduce, but it's not limited to that. We can see how men and women need one another in terms of the characteristics each gender particularly showcases. This is one of the very helpful contributions of early feminism—to point out that "feminine qualities" are as necessary and helpful for human flourishing as male ones. That's not a new insight—it's right there in the first two chapters of Genesis—but it is a truth that was too often ignored, obscured or even outright denied by the church through the ages.

Christianity doesn't sever gender from sex, because according to the Bible, the unique ways that God made our bodies are tied to our gender roles. Humanity's design is tied to humanity's mission. To bring more children into the world, a man and a woman need each other. For a child to know the unique aspects of fathering and mothering, they need to know both a father and mother.

You might have heard someone say, "She complements him nicely." Or, "Those colors really complement the design of this room." What does this mean? It means that without a distinct and different element necessary for its proper fulfillment, something or someone is incomplete. It means that if we're lacking something essential for us to thrive, we'll never experience the full potential that God has equipped us for. This doesn't mean that a person who never marries is somehow incomplete, but it does mean that for humanity as a whole to thrive (in fact, even just to survive), men and women are necessary.

From this, we can say that men and women have a complementary fit. They need one another. We are made, quite literally, to fit together. Think of tongue-and-groove flooring. On their own, each of the two types of flooring wouldn't be capable of being pieced together to make a whole floor. But bring the two types of pieces together, and it becomes (depending on your level of DIY skill) possible for a whole floor to come together—because each type of piece is designed to need the other.

JESUS AND GENDER IDENTITY

Here's what I've said so far...

- God created humanity in his image—we are intentionally made.
- God created humanity in male and female forms—we are not made interchangeable.
- God created humanity in such a way that man and woman are created for one another—each made to complement the other.
- All this was part of God's "very good" blueprint.

None of this, of course, is what the increasingly dominant cultural narrative in Western society says. Increasingly, we find our sense of human worth and what it means to be human without reference to Genesis and outside of being created by God (though it's proving frustratingly hard for people to find it anywhere else).

God made us with the freedom to reject his blueprint. But it's worth finishing this chapter by pointing out that when someone rejects this blueprint, they are not merely rejecting a thousands-of-years-old text.

They are rejecting Jesus.

In the New Testament, Jesus affirms this Genesis account of creation. Here is what he said about humanity, during a debate on the nature and duration of marriage:

> *Have you not read that he who created them from the beginning made them male and female, and said, "Therefore a man shall leave his father and his mother and hold fast to his wife, and the two shall become one flesh"? So they are no longer two but one flesh. What therefore God has joined together, let not man separate. (Matthew 19 v 4-6)*

Jesus is repeating the Genesis pattern for how God designed man and woman. He is quoting Genesis 2 as being true and right. Don't miss what Jesus is saying here:

1. We are created people.
2. We are created male or female.
3. A man is someone who is able to become one flesh—have full sexual intercourse—with a woman, and a woman is someone who is able to become one flesh with a man.
4. What God does, people should not seek to undo.

Of course, this is not all Jesus said and showed about what it means to be human, and to be a man or a woman. Jesus said much more than this—but he did not say less than this. Though it brought him into conflict with some of the prevailing cultural views of first-century Palestine, Jesus taught that Genesis 1 – 2 is God's blueprint. We can ignore Genesis 1 – 2 only if we ignore Jesus.

NO NEED FOR SHAME

Before sin entered the story in Genesis chapter 3, the man and woman were at peace with themselves, one another, and their Creator. Both were living in line with, and as part of, God's blueprint—and it was brilliant:

> *The man and his wife were both naked and were not ashamed. (Genesis 2 v 25)*

Imagine that: a world where everyone is at ease with who they are and how they are made; and feels good about how they look, rather than embarrassed or awkward or deeply disturbed about it; where people are able to completely trust those around them, so that they are able to be open with them. That is a wonderful world. That is the world that, one way and another, many people who sit on both sides of the transgender debate (or in the middle of it) are seeking to cling onto, rediscover, or create.

But it's not possible. Because it's not the world in which we live.

Something happened to the blueprint.

6: BEAUTY AND BROKENNESS

At the end of the last chapter, we left Adam and Eve naked and unashamed. They were living in perfect harmony with one another and with God.

Had the story ended there, the book you have in your hands would not have needed to be written. But the story did not end in Genesis 2 with a "Happily Ever After" picture of Adam and Eve. Paradise didn't stay paradise.

The story took a turn—the chapter of history that is often called "the fall."

Adam and Eve sinned. God had instructed Adam and Eve to not eat of just one tree. Everything else was freely available (Genesis 2 v 15-17).

But Satan offered Eve a pathway of her own choosing, promising her pleasure and enlightenment. Choice had a seductive power long before modern advertising companies were invented. The serpent cast God's rule as restrictive, unfair and petty: "God knows that when you eat of it your eyes will be opened, and you will be like God" (3 v 5).

And so Eve ate of the tree she was instructed not to eat from. Of course, at that moment, it did not seem she was going down the wrong path—because why could denying someone the offer of pleasure and enlightenment be wrong? Eve had seen that "the tree was good for food, and that it was a delight to the eyes, and that the tree was to be desired to make one wise" (v 6). Her decision was a rational, reasonable calculation, supported by what her feelings were saying to her. How could it be wrong when it seemed good, looked delightful, and seemed wise? Especially when her husband agreed and shared the fruit with her.

Isn't that our story, too? We do not cast our decisions to reject what God says as the actions of rebels. We really just see ourselves as owners and masters of ourselves. What could be so wrong?

This is the drama of Genesis 3: the casting off of God's rule. They cast off the role of being God's royal ambassadors assigned to rule over creation in relationship with him, and instead struck out on their own. *You can be like God in your own life,* Satan told the first humans. *You can have the authority. You know what's best. You can't trust God—but you can trust yourself.* And the humans said, *Yes.*

THEIR STORY AND OUR STORY

In reaching for the fruit that represented authority to rule, Adam and Eve denied God's authority, doubted God's knowledge, and disputed God's loving goodness. They would take up the mantle of their own authority; they would see their knowledge as perfect; and they would trust wholly in themselves. They wanted to make the rules for themselves and remold the world to fit a new narrative, one in which they sat on the throne of their lives and they decided what was right and wrong.

This was not just an accidental slip-up; Eve's choice was the choice of an alternative lordship. That is why a seemingly innocent solitary act of eating from the wrong tree put all of creation in a death-spiral. And that is why eating a fruit was an act of treason.

But the Bible's story isn't left in the past tense. It's in the present tense. What occurred in the garden has made its way down to you and me:

> *None is righteous, no, not one; no one understands; no one seeks for God ... no one does good ... there is no fear of God before their eyes. (Romans 3 v 10-11, 12, 18)*

Adam and Eve's story is my story. Adam and Eve's story is your story.

We cannot stand in judgment over Adam and Eve, since each day we choose the same as they did—to sit on the throne by seeking to force God off. And, whoever you are, you cannot point a finger at anyone who disagrees with you when it comes to questions of gender identity. Why? Because we all inhabit a creation marred by sin, and we all contribute to its brokenness by our own sinful choices. We all sin differently, but we all sin, and we are all equal in our sin.

This is our story. And Genesis 3 is a story that does not have a happy ending. In 3 v 7, as soon as they have eaten the fruit, Adam and Eve begin to discover that their choice has not brought enlightenment so much as shame:

> *Then the eyes of both were opened, and they knew that they were naked. And they sewed fig leaves together and made themselves loincloths.*

The first result of the first rejection of God is that people feel ashamed of, and awkward about, their bodies. That is their first experience of living in a world that is now beautiful thanks to its Creator, but broken thanks to their sin.

The first experience, but by no means the only one, nor the worst.

A BROKEN STAGE

Humanity was the highpoint of creation. So it shouldn't surprise us that their rebellion affected the whole of creation:

> *And to Adam [God] said,*
>   *"Because you have listened to the voice of your wife*
> *and have eaten of the tree*
> *of which I commanded you,*
> *'You shall not eat of it,'*
> *cursed is the ground because of you;*
>   *in pain you shall eat of it all the days of your life;*
> *thorns and thistles it shall bring forth for you;*
> *and you shall eat the plants of the field.*
> *By the sweat of your face*
> *you shall eat bread,*
> *till you return to the ground,*
> *for out of it you were taken;*
> *for you are dust,*
>   *and to dust you shall return. (Genesis 3 v 17-19)*

The picture the Bible paints of sin's effects over the world are catastrophic and comprehensive. Creation is broken. The Garden of Eden was a place where work was hard yet fulfilling, because the earth would grow trees that were pleasing to the eye and good for food and free to eat. The cursed world is a place full of thorns and thistles, where work is frustrating and sometimes futile. Floods, tornadoes, and hurricanes are the result of a world thrown into chaos by humanity. We choose to assume God's throne, but we cannot rule his creation.

Humans break. We are dust, and we are frail and failing. Cancer. Depression. Eating disorders. Heart disease. Gender dysphoria. Each of these painful realities testifies to the brokenness of creation. And that is before we add the pain caused by moral failures, whether on a global scale (the Holocaust) or a familial one (domestic violence, neglect).

Humans die. The penalty of sin is death (Romans 6 v 23). We shall return to the dust from which we were taken—and that reality overshadows our lives, giving a sense of futility to all our efforts and mocking all our achievements and accumulations. And we face an eternity outside Eden, outside the perfection of God's presence. This is the worst consequence of our sin.

We are broken actors living on a broken stage, and we do not stand on the stage for very long.

To think about gender dysphoria or transgenderism in a way that listens hard and humbly to God, we need to let him tell us that this world is not how it was intended to be—and why. And we need to understand that the effects of the fall are not only around us but within us. That is going to be really hard—but as you read, please be aware that we finish this chapter with a promise of hope, and that the next chapter (and the rest of the book) is all about that hope. This chapter is not the end of this book and the fall is not the end of our story.

WHAT HAPPENED TO OUR HEARTS

Beloved, I urge you as sojourners and exiles to abstain from the passions of the flesh, which wage war against your soul. (1 Peter 2 v 11)

Inside every heart, there's a war; and the heart is both the victim and the culprit. Why? Because every person's heart is inhabited by sinful desires, and produces sinful desires. There is an ongoing battle within the heart in which unhelpful desires wage war with our conscience.

Bitterness. Anger. Envy. Greed. We cannot trust our feelings or all the passions that reside within us simply because we feel them. Our hearts are not pure—far from it:

> *The heart is deceitful above all things, and desperately sick; who can understand it? (Jeremiah 17 v 9)*

The nature of deception is to convince us that our hearts will not be satisfied unless we indulge what our hearts desire. But our hearts lead us astray in countless ways. Envy robs people of joy and contentment, sours friendships, and can lead to compromising morality in order to "get ahead." Envy does not produce flourishing or joy in people. Indulging envy only results in misery for yourself and others. But none of us think this way as envy rages on. In the moment, the wrath and bitterness of envy assuages the sense of loss and jealousy residing within each of us.

Not every impulse we experience should be indulged. We should be suspicious about "listening to our hearts." Actually, everyone knows this is true. Prisons are full of people who acted in accord with their feelings—and who have been told by society that they shouldn't. Every time a therapist tells a patient to view themselves more positively, they are accepting that there are feelings that are unhelpful to someone's fulfillment. Our hearts' desires can be at war with what is actually good for our hearts. The real question is: which desires should be fed, and which should be starved?

What does this have to do with transgenderism? In the same way that fallen desires pervade the hearts of all of us, individuals with gender dysphoria experience real feelings of distress about their gender identity. These are authentic experiences, where their heart's desire is telling them one thing about themselves while their body is saying something else. No one should dismiss this, or belittle this, or joke about this. To feel this way is to experience real, deep pain.

But experiencing that feeling does not mean that feeding it and acting upon it is best, or right. The impulse to live out an identity at odds with our biological sex is to indulge fallen desires that our heart believes will bring peace. But internal longing for peace does not mean that finding peace is possible through breaking the boundaries of human limitations and rejecting the way we have each been created. It is a little-reported fact that people who undergo sex re-assignment surgery do not, statistically, report higher levels of happiness after the surgery.[14] That is, acting on the desire to live as the opposite gender to the one that accords with biological sex does not bring peace to a heart. This is consistent with a "Genesis 1 – 3" worldview, because the Bible tells us that embracing a desire at odds with the Creator's design will never bring ultimate happiness. The passion to live as a member of the opposite sex isn't simply satisfied by surgically altering your body. There are deeper issues at stake than exterior, physical and cosmetic alterations.

GENDER DYSPHORIA IS NOT SINFUL

It is vital to pause here to make very clear a distinction between experiencing a feeling and acting on a feeling. Come back to Eve in Eden at the start of Genesis 3. Eve was not

---

14 Paul McHugh, "Transgender Surgery Isn't the Solution," *Wall Street Journal*, May 13, 2016, www.wsj.com/articles/paul-mchugh-transgender-surgery-isnt-the-solution-1402615120.

sinning when Satan spoke to her to tempt her, when she saw the fruit's beauty, or when she felt it was to be desired. She sinned when she went beyond observing the fruit's beauty, followed her reason and feelings in opposition to God's word, and took and ate it.

In the same way, individuals who experience gender dysphoria are not sinning when such experiences occur. To feel that your body is one sex and your self is a different gender is not sinful. The Bible nowhere categorizes unwanted psychological distress as sinful in itself. This experience is a sign that all of our selves are as broken by sin as the creation around us is. The reason that any person ever experiences a physical ailment or a psychological state or perception that goes against God's creative intentions is because creation itself is fallen. So, for example, while having cancer or depression—or experiencing gender dysphoria—is not sinful, these experiences occur because this is a world broken by sin.

But deciding to let that feeling rule—to feed that feeling so that it becomes the way you see yourself and the way you identify yourself and the way you act—is sinful, because it is deciding that your feelings will have authority over you, and will define what is right and what is wrong. It is to act in the same way Adam and Eve did in eating from the tree.

THINKING IT THROUGH

When our hearts are hardened—when we have decided not to love God or to treat him as God—our minds are affected, too. That is, not only our feelings and desires, but also our logic and reason are touched by sin. In speaking of the difference it makes to live under God's authority rather than how those who live in rejection of God's right to rule ("Gentiles") do, Paul says:

*You must no longer walk as the Gentiles do, in the futility
of their minds. They are darkened in their understanding,
alienated from the life of God because of the ignorance
that is in them, due to their hardness of heart.*

(*Ephesians 4 v 17-18*)

Without God in the picture, our reason is impaired. We can think brilliantly, but not necessarily truthfully. Our reason is flawed, because it leaves out the Creator in trying to understand his creation and ourselves as his image-bearing creatures. We grope around for answers that cannot be found, like blundering around in the dark in the middle of the night, trying to find the light switch in a room without switches.

In many ways, the heart and mind work in tandem. Our hearts can have a pull or attraction or desire toward one thing, but our mind might know that such attraction or desire should not be acted upon. Equally, our mind often seeks to justify the decisions of our hearts. This explains why individuals like the atheist scholar Richard Dawkins can be both very clever and very blind—because his cleverness is all being used in the service of his determination to reject God. His logic is actually just following the decision of his heart to be hard to God.

Our minds matter in the transgender debate because it is the mind that processes the experiences of those who suffer gender dysphoria. If you like, our minds tell our hearts whether our feelings are reasonable. But just as with our desires, in a world broken by sin we cannot be sure whether our mind's reasoning is valid. It is not intrinsically more reasonable to follow the feelings of your heart than to reject the feelings of your heart.

CAN A MAN CHANGE HIS HEIGHT?

It is worth following through the logic that is used to validate the view that how I feel about who I am should trump what my body says about who I am. A viral video from 2016 shows a young Caucasian man in his thirties interviewing college students at an American university, and demonstrates the slippery slope of taking the implications of transgender ideology to its logical conclusions.[15] He first asks a variety of students how they would respond to him telling them he is a woman. The replies include:

"Good for you."

"I'd be like, what? Really?"

"I don't have a problem with it."

Next, he asks how they would respond to him claiming to be Chinese...

"I might be a little surprised but I would say, 'Good for you!' Yeah, be who you are."

"I would maybe think you had some Chinese ancestor."

"Umm, I would have a lot of questions—just because on the outside I would assume you are a white man."

The next questions are whether the students would be happy with the interviewer claiming to be seven years old and seeking to enroll in a school class for seven-year-olds, a first-grade class. This time, there is more hesitation among the students—but the answers include:

"I probably wouldn't believe it but, I mean, it wouldn't really bother me that much [that I would] go out of my

---

15 Family Policy Institute of Washington, "College Kids Say the Darndest Things," April 13, 2016. Available at www.youtube.com/watch?v=xfO1veFs6Ho.

way and tell you, 'No, you are wrong.' I'd just be like, 'Oh, he wants to be seven years old.'"

"If you feel seven at heart, then so be it—good for you."

"If [first grade] is where you feel mentally you should be then I feel like there are communities that would accept you for that."

"I would say, so long as you are not hindering society and you're not causing harm to other people, I feel like [joining first grade] should be an okay thing.

Lastly, the interviewer asks the same students what they would say if he told them he was 6 feet 5 inches tall— around 10 inches taller than he appears to be.

STUDENT ONE: (No answer.)

STUDENT TWO: That I would question.

INTERVIEWER: Why?

STUDENT TWO: Because you're not. No, I don't think you're 6'5".

STUDENT THREE: If you truly believed you're 6'5", I don't think its harmful. I think it's fine if you believe that. It doesn't matter to me if you think you are taller than you are.

INTERVIEWER: So you'd be willing to tell me I'm wrong?

STUDENT THREE: No, I wouldn't tell you you are wrong.

STUDENT ONE: No, but I'd say that, umm, I don't think that you are.

STUDENT FOUR: I feel like that's not my place as another human to say someone is wrong or to draw lines or boundaries.

STUDENT FIVE: No, I mean I wouldn't just go like, "Oh, you're wrong," like that's wrong to believe in it. Because again, it doesn't really bother me what you want to think about your height or anything.
INTERVIEWER: So I can be a Chinese woman?
STUDENT TWO: Umm, sure.
INTERVIEWER: But I can't be a 6'5" Chinese woman?
STUDENT SIX: Yes.
STUDENT SEVEN: If you thoroughly debated me or explained why you felt your were 6'5", uhh, I feel like I would be very open to saying you were 6'5" or Chinese or a woman.

Deciding that the only reasonable course of action is to affirm every feeling about self-identity that someone has is a blind alley that leads to absurdity. Worse, it is dangerous. In the transgender debate, the argument is that we must accept the claim that a man who identifies as a woman is really a woman. But work that backwards on a different example: would it be kind to tell someone suffering from anorexia that their self-perception of being overweight is correct simply because that is how they perceive themselves? Or would it be kind to tell someone who feels as though their life is not worth living, and whose mind feels those feelings are reasonable, that they should act on what their heart and head are saying? Absolutely not. That would be cruel, not kind.

THE WAY WE'RE PUT TOGETHER

There is one more personal aspect of living in a world broken by sin that we must consider:

> To the woman [God] said,
> "I will surely multiply your pain in childbearing;

in pain you shall bring forth children" ...
And to Adam he said ...
You are dust, and to dust you will return. "
(Genesis 3 v 16, 17, 19)

Physical pain is a part of life from the moment we enter this world through childbirth. And from birth onward, we're on the slow journey back to what we are made of: dust. Between birth and death, no one enjoys a body that works as they wish it would, and as it should. The way we are put together is no more immune from the effects of the fall than the way our hearts feel or the way our minds reason.

This means that arguing, "I was born this way," sounds compelling, but is not ultimately a clinching argument. All of us have characteristics that we have always had and that we ourselves wish we could change, or that our society, or our family, or some of our friends tell us we should wish to change. In one way or another, we are all "born that way"—but we're born that way in broken bodies. People are born with all sorts of predispositions that do not produce joy and wholeness. The way I was born still requires evaluation to determine whether that "way" is a positive one, to be affirmed, embraced and lived out; or a negative one, to be rejected, moderated, or treated. If I am born with a predisposition toward aggression, Western culture would not tell me, "Go for it—you were born that way, there's nothing you can do about it" (though many societies 2,000 years ago may well have done). Whatever "we are born with" is to be evaluated by Scripture.

The same is true for people who experience gender dysphoria. One prominent theory about what "causes" gender dysphoria is what's called the brain-sex theory. This concept states that individuals with gender dysphoria have a brain structure that mimics the brain-type of the opposite sex. Evidence is inconclusive on this, however, meaning that currently there is no known cause for gender dysphoria. This is at best a hypothesis. But our bodies are broken—what we are born with is not necessarily what we are created to live out.

THE BLUEPRINT PERSISTS

So how should we think about gender fluidity and transgenderism? The feeling or experience of it is not sinful, but it is broken; and acting upon one's dysphoria is sinful.

And the act is doomed to frustration. Even in a Genesis 3 world, the Genesis 1 blueprint persists. God has not given up on his creation and he does not let us rip up his blueprint. Whatever the perceptions and desires that we experience internally, an objective order exists that our biology attests to.

So when Adam and Eve grasped at being gods instead of humans, acting as Creator rather than creatures, God did not allow them to have what they wanted in full. They did not cease to be creatures under God's rule simply because they had decided not to live that way anymore. They did not become divine, or self-ruling. That lay outside their reach.

We can grasp at being men instead of women—or genderless humans instead of gendered humans—but God does not allow it. We are unable to do it. We can change our form, but we cannot change our formatting. In truth, there is no such thing as "transgender," because you cannot change your gender. The word exists, but not the reality that it seeks to describe.

As Paul McHugh states:

> *"Transgendered men do not become women, nor do transgendered women become men. All (including Bruce Jenner)*

become feminized men or masculinized women, counterfeits or impersonators of the sex with which they 'identify.'" [16]

Many would be outraged by that statement—so it is worth noting that Paul McHugh is one of the most esteemed psychiatrists of our time. He serves as the University Distinguished Professor of Psychiatry at Johns Hopkins Medical School and was the former psychiatrist-in-chief at Johns Hopkins Hospital. He offered these remarks on how to assess the transgender movement:

"In fact, gender dysphoria—the official psychiatric term for feeling oneself to be of the opposite sex—belongs in the family of similarly disordered assumptions about the body, such as anorexia nervosa and body dysmorphic disorder. Its treatment should not be directed at the body as with surgery and hormones any more than one treats obesity-fearing anorexic patients with liposuction. The treatment should strive to correct the false, problematic nature of the assumption and to resolve the psychosocial conflicts provoking it." [17]

As the author Tony Reinke has written:

"Chromosomes cannot be re-engineered, removed, or scrubbed from the software of our bodies. It may be possible for a 'trans woman' to 'pass' for a woman on the street at the visual level, but it is not possible for a man to morph himself into a biological woman, with all the experiences and functions of natural femaleness. The biological narrative doesn't exist. While medical advances

---

16 "Transgenderism: A Pathogenic Meme," *The Public Discourse,* June 10, 2015, www.thepublicdiscourse.com/2015/06/15145.
17 As previous.

> *make it possible to suppress or change some of the out-*
> *ward appearances of our bodies, and change our patterns*
> *of speech and dress, it is not possible to raze our bodies*
> *to the ground and rebuild them without shortcutting all*
> *the essential formative experiences that make the biological*
> *sex expression and gender authentic.*
>
> *"A 'trans woman' can grow his hair long and wear high-*
> *heels and pump estrogen into his body. And a 'trans man'*
> *can cut her hair short, and force testosterone into her body.*
> *All of this is an active pushing against the body's internal*
> *software. Unable to decode ourselves from the genetics of*
> *our physical becoming, we are left to rearrange anatomi-*
> *cal aesthetics and coerce ourselves in a direction that runs*
> *against nature."* [18]

This is a bleak picture of humanity and the world—every part of which is marked and marred by sin. It's hard to read if you or a loved one are experiencing gender dysphoria, or are in the midst of or out the other side of hormone treatment or surgery. But in fact, it should actually be hard for *all* of us to read—because we all suffer from living in a fallen world, and we all contribute to its fallenness. We all sin. To transition is *a* sin—but it is not *the* sin; it is not worse than lust, adultery, envy, greed, and all those other sins that middle-class heterosexual guys try to explain away or excuse themselves for. We all coerce ourselves in a direction that runs against nature each time we seek to sit on God's throne.

The person who feels morally superior or self-righteous at the sins of others—including those who have followed

---

18 "All of Us Sinners, None of Us Freaks: Christian Convictions for the Transgender Age," *Desiring God,* August 6, 2016. Available at: www.desiringgod.org/articles/all-of-us-sinners-none-of-us-freaks.

the transgender path—is feeding a feeling that wars against their own soul no less than the person who would like to be of the opposite sex. Jesus' strongest words were reserved for those who defined themselves by comparing themselves favorably with others, and who felt their own goodness was enough to earn them approval from God.

WE ARE NOT LEFT WHERE WE ARE

This is a beautiful world. But it is also a broken one. And it is filled with humans who are capable of great good and of great mistakes, who can reach great heights but who are fundamentally flawed. Our hearts, our minds, and our bodies are beautiful things, and they are broken things. They have been since Adam and Eve first decided they would be better rulers of this creation than its Creator.

But there is hope buried in brokenness. In the same chapter where humanity descends into an abyss of sin and brokenness, God announces in germ form the promise to rescue his image-bearers:

> *The* LORD *God said to the serpent…*
> *"I will put enmity between you and the woman,*
>   *and between your offspring and her offspring;*
> *he shall bruise your head,*
>   *and you shall bruise his heel." (Genesis 3 v 14, 15)*

God does not leave us where we are. God promises to send someone into where we are to lead us out…

7. A BETTER FUTURE

A 2016 issue of *Time* magazine featured an essay by Jessi Hempel telling the heart-wrenching story of her brother, Evan, giving birth to a son.[19]

That sentence might catch you off guard. (If it didn't, maybe read it again, a little slower!)

The photo the story features shows what looks like a man breastfeeding an infant son. Titled "My Brother's Pregnancy and the Making of a New American Family," Hempel recounts how her sister underwent a female-to-male transition at 19, but still desired to give birth—and did so at 35.

She describes the long-ago transition that included testosterone injections, producing thick hair over her sister's knuckles. At that time, Evan elected not to have breast-removal surgery, thus making possible what is called "chestfeeding."

The story is not without several painful admissions. Recounting how much they once looked alike, Hempel laments the loss of her sister's feminine appearance. And at one point, Hempel observes that Evan, while pregnant, experienced a "traumatizing disconnect between his masculinity and the female attributes of his body."

---

19 www.time.com/4475634/trans-man-pregnancy-evan/

She asks a question that helpfully frames how Christians should begin thinking about the transgender revolution: "What if you are born into a female body, know you are a man, and still want to participate in the traditionally exclusive rite of womanhood? What kind of man are you then?"

That question touches on a quest we all know: the search for resolution and satisfaction, for a life of equilibrium, without heartache or alienation or disconnect.

It's understandable that Evan would assume that it's only by following our feelings that we can find this. Understandable, but incorrect, as Evan—according to Jessi's article—discovered through personal experience. Evan found in life what we saw in the last chapter: you don't break free from the effects of the fall by following the course of the fall in your own life and decisions.

Is there hope for individuals like Evan? Can those who face the same kind of struggles find wholeness, and experience psychological relief, bodily relief, and emotional relief? Given the reality of the fall, is there good news for us, regardless of what brokenness each person experiences, regardless of what identities we embrace?

Yes!

The Bible's message to the person struggling with gender-identity issues is the same for the person struggling with envy or depression or anything else:

> *If anyone is in Christ, he is a new creation. The old has passed away; behold, the new has come.*
> *(2 Corinthians 5 v 17)*

Here is the offer God holds out to every single one of us: *you can be a new creation.*

To become a new creation in Christ does not mean the world we live in, or the bodies we inhabit, or the minds we think with will be totally freed and completely healed. To be a new creation in Christ is to experience the promise of what fully awaits those who place their trust in him—to be able to anticipate the certainty of a coming day when the disorder of creation is put back together, and when dysphoria of any kind is replaced by euphoria of every kind. To be a new creation is to know why the world is the way it is, why our bodies are the way they are, and why our minds think as they do. It is to be equipped with the power of God's Holy Spirit to live in relationship with God. A new creation in Christ recognizes that even in broken minds living in broken bodies living in a broken world, there is a definitive and clear "very good" blueprint of creation.

A new creation has ceased to belong to this "old," fallen world, even as they live in it, for they are walking toward the full newness of a renewed, re-perfected world.

We saw in the last chapter that the fall affects our hearts, minds and bodies—and in this chapter we'll see how the gospel offers us freedom and hope in each of those areas. That's what this chapter addresses.

WAITING FOR FREEDOM

As we saw in the last chapter, we live in a broken creation marred by sin. But wonderfully, this is not the final state of this world:

> *For I consider that the sufferings of this present time are not worth comparing with the glory that is to be revealed to us. For the creation waits with eager longing for the revealing of the sons of God. For the creation was subjected*

*to futility, not willingly, but because of him who subjected
it, in hope that the creation itself will be set free from its
bondage to corruption and obtain the freedom of the glory
of the children of God. For we know that the whole creation has been groaning together in the pains of childbirth
until now. And not only the creation, but we ourselves,
who have the firstfruits of the Spirit, groan inwardly as
we wait eagerly for adoption as sons, the redemption of our
bodies. For in this hope we were saved. Now hope that is
seen is not hope. For who hopes for what he sees? But if we
hope for what we do not see, we wait for it with patience.*

(Romans 8 v 18-25)

"Redemption" means the act of being set free. It's a release from "bondage to corruption." As he writes to those
who are new creations living in this broken creation, Paul
does not pit suffering and redemption against one another in total contrast. They are experienced simultaneously,
because redemption is an eternal promise that has broken
into the present, but has not yet been fulfilled in the present. A Christian is free to look beyond all that makes them
groan, but right now they are not free from what makes
them groan.

There are several truths in this passage of great signifi-
cance for someone who experiences gender dysphoria.

First, it reminds us that the world around us "groans."
The sense of trauma, of alienation, of discomfort that results from gender dysphoria has an explanation: a world
under sin's curse.

Second, Romans 8 teaches us that "we ourselves" groan.
Paul is narrowing the focus. It isn't just that an abstract
idea of "creation" is groaning; we are all subject to groaning because all is not well within and around us.

Third, we are assured that our groans are not eternal.

Both God's creation and everyone who is a new creation are heading toward ultimate hope and glory. There is a way to groan with hope, because one day we will be set free. We await the "redemption of our bodies" at the moment when all of creation is "set free from its bondage to corruption" and everything is put right. There is a way back to Eden, to a perfect world. That is not where creation is now, but it is where creation is heading. The arc of history bends toward hope.

Gender dysphoria is a deep, painful struggle, causing pain, anguish, and tears. But it is not the only struggle. The whole world struggles; the whole world cries out, one way or another. The good news of the gospel is that those groans have been heard and those groans need not last. As adopted sons and daughters of God, our gnawing sense of despair about the world or about ourselves is met with a promise that someday—someday—God is going to renew creation. So not only will the feelings of dysphoria be removed, but the conditions that give rise to dysphoria in the first place will be eradicated as well.

The gospel does not promise that any of us will experience this freedom, this sense of wholeness and rightness, right now. We are waiting, which means the person with dysphoria may never know a life apart from dysphoria until God restores creation. They may not know it until Christ brings them to heaven, or returns to bring heaven to earth. But they will know it.

So the Bible acknowledges how things are, even in the deepest and darkest moments—but it also promises that we need not be left there. It teaches us to groan, but to groan with hope—to acknowledge the brokenness and to cling to the escape from the brokenness that God has provided.

THINKING CLEARLY

Though the brokenness does not stop as soon as we let our groans lead us to faith, the Spirit of God does start to make a difference to the way we live with and think about, that brokenness. One way is by bringing clarity to our minds:

> *For those who live according to the flesh set their minds on the things of the flesh, but those who live according to the Spirit set their minds on the things of the Spirit. For to set the mind on the flesh is death, but to set the mind on the Spirit is life and peace. (Romans 8 v 5-6)*

"The flesh" is a way of describing the way the world works, in which we focus on the desires we experience and live them out. Faith in Christ offers a different way: to experience God's Spirit enabling us to live with our minds set on his "things"—his truth, his discernment, and his wisdom. Our thinking is no longer stuck in the grooves of a fallen mind.

So, for instance…

> *We know that the whole creation has been groaning together in the pains of childbirth until now. And not only the creation, but we ourselves, who have the firstfruits of the Spirit, groan inwardly as we wait eagerly for adoption as sons, the redemption of our bodies. (v 22-23)*

The Spirit enables us to "know" the predicament that creation and humanity are in. It is he who helps us to think, "I am groaning, but I am also waiting for a time when I will no longer groan." He teaches us to view our bodies as broken but valuable, and as part of a blueprint that we did not draw.

The Spirit helps us to see what is true, and that what is true is good, even as our feelings (or "flesh") tell us something else.

In some ways, having our minds set by, and on, the Spirit can make things harder because it awakens us to the reality that we are engaged in a spiritual battle. Think about it(!): if I could just indulge my lust, rather than battling it, life would be easier. If I could just give vent to my anger, rather than seeking to combat it with love and patience, life would be less tiring. But it would also be less satisfying than living in line with God's plan.

With this renewed mind, it becomes possible to rightly evaluate our own feelings, and the opinions of our culture:

> *Do not be conformed to this world, but be transformed by the renewal of your mind, that by testing you may discern what is the will of God, what is good and acceptable and perfect. (Romans 12 v 2)*

God re-orders how we reason. No longer will someone fall prey to the idea that it might just be possible for a Caucasian man to become a Chinese woman.

A CHANGE OF HEART

As well as renewing our minds, the Spirit changes our hearts. Six centuries before the life, death and resurrection of his Son, God had promised that as a result of his coming:

> *I will give you a new heart, and a new spirit I will put within you. And I will remove the heart of stone from your flesh and give you a heart of flesh. And I will put my Spirit within you, and cause you to walk in my statutes and be careful to obey my rules. (Ezekiel 36 v 26-27)*

This is God's promise about what happens when someone becomes a Christian (not what happens at some stage after you become a Christian).

A "heart of stone" is describing the heart that most loves something other than God. A "heart of flesh" is one that is alive to God, which loves God, and which therefore obeys God, not out of a sense of having to, but of deep-down wanting to. (Confusingly, Jeremiah uses the word "flesh" very differently than Paul does!) It's still a struggle because we are not perfect, and we still experience our old desires—but the crucial difference is that a "heart of flesh" now has knowing God as its greatest desire, and pleasing him as its greatest aim. Our identity lies in being God's. It is possible to desire to live as God wants, out of love for him, even as we experience other feelings that suggest that we should live as he does not want.

This means that someone who is struggling with gender dysphoria is able to see their struggles with dysphoria from the proper perspective. The struggles are real and afflicting and painful—but they are not the defining aspect of who that person is. That person's identity lies in being a child of God, walking towards being home with him. Their feelings are not a barrier to experiencing joy.

God doesn't promise to eliminate those feelings as long as we are in our earthly bodies, but the gospel has the power to equip us to understand and respond to those feelings with the truth of God's word. The Bible neither explicitly nor implicitly promises that the Spirit will change or lessen someone's experience of gender dysphoria. God may do that; or he may make it so the desire to please him is stronger than the desire to act on one's dysphoria.

A (BETTER) FUTURE FOR OUR BODIES

In the new creation, there will no longer be sadness or death. Brokenness will be no more. The cancer and the tsunamis that plow over humanity—GONE:

> *Then I saw a new heaven and a new earth, for the first heaven and the first earth had passed away, and the sea was no more. And I saw the holy city, new Jerusalem, coming down out of heaven from God, prepared as a bride adorned for her husband. And I heard a loud voice from the throne saying, "Behold, the dwelling place of God is with man. He will dwell with them, and they will be his people, and God himself will be with them as their God. He will wipe away every tear from their eyes, and death shall be no more, neither shall there be mourning, nor crying, nor pain anymore, for the former things have passed away." (Revelation 21 v 1-4)*

This promise is what Evan, with whose story we begin this chapter is searching for. What Evan and everyone who is transgender are looking for—and what everyone who thinks they may be transgender and everyone who knows they are not are looking for—is a way to make their mind's perception, their heart's desires, and their body's construction "match"—to feel wholeness, rather than dysphoria. And that's exactly what the gospel promises—not by us seeking to transition from one sex to another (which is impossible), but by waiting; not by us tearing up the blueprint rebelliously, but by living faithfully and patiently, even though it's painful, until one day there will be transformation. Unlike the partial, frustrating, and ultimately unfulfilling and conflicting transformations that the world offers, this is real, joyful, complete and fulfilling transformation. This is what the Christian is waiting for:

We await a Savior, the Lord Jesus Christ, who will trans-
form our lowly body to be like his glorious body, by the
power that enables him even to subject all things to himself.
                                    (Philippians 3 v 20-21)

How brilliant it is to think of God one day saying to the person with gender dysphoria who waited faithfully, *Well done. I know it's been so hard. It's over now. I love you so much that I have brought you to a place where who you feel you are, and who you truly are, are completely enmeshed. There will be no more pain or crying for you anymore. What you longed for—to feel like, look like, and be the same person—is reality. I know it's been painful. It won't be now. Well done, faithful follower.*

We live in a Genesis 3 world with a Genesis 1 blueprint on the trajectory to a Revelation 21 future.

JESUS IS THE WAY

The path to that life in that world is through putting our faith in Jesus, the Son of God. Why? Because...

There is therefore now no condemnation for those who are in Christ Jesus. For the law of the Spirit of life has set you free in Christ Jesus from the law of sin and death. For God has done what the law, weakened by the flesh, could not do. By sending his own Son in the likeness of sinful flesh and for sin, he condemned sin in the flesh, in order that the righteous requirement of the law might be fulfilled in us, who walk not according to the flesh but according to the Spirit. (Romans 8 v 1-4)

The way to that world was opened up by God "sending his own Son." He frees us from condemnation, which is the greatest freedom we need, and the freedom which brings us all other freedoms (v 1).

This freedom is found only in him. There is no freedom, in this life or in the next, in walking "according to the flesh"—that is, in following our feelings wherever they take us. Equally, there is no freedom in seeking to obey God's blueprint in our own strength—our flesh is too weak and our flesh cannot change itself. Freedom does not lie in indulging those feelings, but neither does it come from simply seeking to ignore them. It lies in being open about them, and coming to Christ with them to find forgiveness, freedom, and openness to the confidence that Jesus is powerful enough to bring sustaining hope in our darkest, most difficult hours. He does not snuff out smoldering wicks.

Only Jesus can offer this kind of freedom because only Jesus could do what we cannot. He lived the perfect, image-reflecting life that we have not. And he died to bear the consequences for our sin—the death and condemnation everyone deserves for deciding to deny the goodness of God, dispute his right to rule, and destroy his image in them. God put all of our rebellion, all of our sin, all of the creation's disorder onto Jesus. The perfect Son of God was treated as a sinner—no one ever experienced greater dysphoria than the perfect Son of God being treated like a sinner at the cross. In suffering this, he brought us into relationship with the God we had rejected, and brought his Spirit into our lives to inspire, strengthen and change us. The Spirit "has set you free from the law of sin and death." This doesn't mean that our lives will be marked by total sinlessness, but that the Spirit of God works in our hearts to set us free from sin's power over us.

The story of Jesus did not end with death, but with resurrection—not with suffering, but with glory. The resurrection was God's act of vindicating Jesus' claim of being a King; and the resurrection was the breaking of the new creation into the present. And the new creation grows each time someone comes to Jesus, in faith, for forgiveness, life, and help.

TRANSFORMATION

So the answer to the person struggling with gender dysphoria is the same as to the person struggling with any other product of the fall—there is hope, there can be change, and there will one day be total transformation.

And the answer to the person who has acted on their gender dysphoria, seeking to tear up the blueprint, is the same as to the person who has torn it up in any other way (which is all of us)—another took the fall for that, bore the condemnation for that rebellion, and offers you freedom.

Let me finish this chapter by taking you back to Evan's story. The question that Evan's sister wondered aloud about—the question of contentment, joy, and self-acceptance in place of the disconnect—is a question that plagues every human heart. The culture around us answers those questions with a million different and conflicting responses. Christians have only one answer to give, but it is all the answer anyone needs, and it is an answer that we must continue to believe in and hold out: *Jesus came and died and rose in order to offer you his Spirit today, and to offer you the life you are searching for in the future.*

The Lord Jesus, and the future he offers, make sense of the suffering in and around us now; and his Spirit strengthens anyone, no matter how hard their life is, to struggle on with joy now, knowing that what is to come for Jesus' family is what they most want to experience—the glory and peace of perfection:

For I consider that the sufferings of this present time are not worth comparing with the glory that is to be revealed to us. (Romans 8 v 18)

Jesus is where we find what we are looking for. The Christian answer is not a restrictive command, but a better story: a story that actually works.

8. LOVE YOUR NEIGHBOR

Love can never be an optional extra for a Christian. To be a Christian means to love as you have been loved by God:

> *A new commandment I give to you, that you love one another: just as I have loved you, you also are to love one another. By this all people will know that you are my disciples, if you have love for one another. (John 13 v 34-35)*

Did you catch that? Jesus says that if we fail to love others, we show we do not really love God. And his famous parable of the Good Samaritan shows that by others, he means all others (Luke 10:25-37). My neighbor includes anyone and everyone.

Jesus' apostle John spells it out:

> *If anyone says, "I love God," and hates his brother, he is a liar; for he who does not love his brother whom he has seen cannot love God whom he has not seen. (1 John 4 v 20)*

For followers of Christ, love is not just an attitude tacked on to the Christian life as an afterthought. Love is not an appetizer or a dessert; love is the main course. A heart that cultivates love for God and love toward others is at the core of what it means to be a Christian. Jesus even says that the love we foster in our hearts toward others is a reflection of the love we have for God. You cannot be a Christian and harbor hatred toward others, because love is the foundation of the greatest commandments:

> *Jesus answered, "The most important [commandment] is,*
> *"Hear, O Israel: The Lord our God, the Lord is one.*
> *And you shall love the Lord your God with all your heart*
> *and with all your soul and with all your mind and with*
> *all your strength." The second is this: "You shall love your*
> *neighbor as yourself." There is no other commandment*
> *greater than these." (Mark 12 v 29-31)*

The centrality of love must be the foundation for our interaction with friends, family, neighbors, and fellow citizens—including all those who are experiencing gender dysphoria or who have embraced a transgender identity.

A biblical response to transgender people is to see them as our neighbors; and then to love them, because they are our neighbors. But this is easier said than done, even if we are determined to turn our back on unloving, knee-jerk reactions of one kind or another. From the Bible to the Beatles, we're told that "all you need is love"—but what does it actually mean to love someone? I may want to act lovingly toward all people, regardless of their race, age, background, or gender identity—but how do I do that?

LOVE PROMOTES DIGNITY

First, we need to understand who our neighbors are: people made in God's image, as we've already seen:

> *God created man in his own image,*
> *in the image of God he created him;*
> *male and female he created them. (Genesis 1 v 27)*

The truth that man and woman are made in God's image is the foundation for human dignity—the concept that individuals possess an inviolable worth, deserving of honor and respect. There are no exception clauses to this truth; there is no way for someone to be a human and not bear God's image, even though they may obscure or mar it. Nothing they can do with their lives, or do to their lives, can eradicate the image of God. No human authority can take it away. All humans possess God-given dignity, and possess it equally.

President or peasants—both are exactly the same in God's eyes. Christian or non-Christian—both are made in God's image. Gay or straight—both possess the same inherent dignity. A person confused about their gender and someone at peace with their gender—both possess the same dignity.

Failing to understand how this truth applies to every single person equally is at the foundation for all sorts of abuse and atrocities.

- In Nazi Germany, a failure to see the full dignity of Jews lead to the Holocaust.
- At the founding of the US, a failure on the part of most white people to see the full dignity of persons with black skin led to the evils of racism and slavery.
- For the last fifty years, a failure to see the full dignity of persons who are not yet born has led to fifty million legal abortions in the US alone.

History's greatest crimes result from denying God's image in every single man and woman.

A transgendered person is made in God's image, and that means that respect and honor are due to them as people, regardless of whether we agree with their self-perception.

To see the full dignity of a transgendered person means to abhor or reject any mocking humor that would demean them. It means to stand up and defend them against bullies or abuse. Dignity demands that we speak up in the defense of someone's worth, even when we disagree with their way of life.

LOVE REQUIRES EMPATHY

Understanding the perspective of someone unlike you is absolutely vital to developing empathy and building relationships. Empathy is the prerequisite for speaking meaningfully and authoritatively into someone's life.

Paul tells the church in Galatia to…

> *Bear one another's burdens, and so fulfill the law of Christ. (Galatians 6 v 2)*

To love someone, we must work hard to empathize with them. And that means seeking to look at life from their perspective and walk in their shoes:

> *"You cannot help with a burden unless you come very close to the burdened person … so in the same way, a Christian must listen and understand, and physically, emotionally, spiritually, take up some of the burden with the other person."* [20]

---

20 Timothy Keller, *Galatians For You* (The Good Book Company, 2013), page 168.

To take one example, at one point in her life my wife did not understand the challenges and concerns of African Americans, which led her to dismiss those concerns as unwarranted. She was not racist, but she simply did not understand the perspective of someone of that ethnicity. It wasn't until she became friends with an African-American woman in our church that she gained an appreciation and sensitivity for understanding why people different than her perceive the world differently than she does.

So we need to ask ourselves, "Have I actually made an effort to understand the perspective and pain of someone experiencing gender dysphoria?"

This is why it is crucial to read testimonies of people who experience dysphoria; to make more effort, not less, to befriend someone in your neighborhood who lives out a gender identity different than their biological sex; and never to dismiss them out of hand because their struggles seem alien or strange to you, or because you disagree with the choices they have made or the identity they have assumed.

Extending empathy does not mean that you accept or affirm or encourage someone to embrace the desire to live contrary to their created gender; it does mean, however, that instead of rejecting a person outright, you take time and make the effort to listen and seek to understand.

There are going to be people in our lives who experience gender dysphoria. It is inevitable. They will be in our churches, in our families and in our schools. What are you doing now to cultivate a spirit of tenderness? What are you going to do when you encounter someone who admits to these struggles? Will you respond with your jaw on the floor? Will your facial reaction turn someone away, or will you extend a hand or a hug of friendship, and make sure you ask questions and listen hard? What our eyebrows and noses do when we meet someone tells them much more about how we truly feel than our fine words or our reflective blogs.

The Bible says we are not only to get to know people, but we are to bear their burdens—which means someone's struggles become our struggles. You cannot love your neighbor if you will not empathize with them.

LOVE SHARES TRUTH

[Love] does not rejoice at wrongdoing, but rejoices with the truth. (1 Corinthians 13 v 6)

Here is perhaps the most delicate aspect of loving our transgender neighbor: how can we love our transgender neighbor while not sending signals that we approve of someone living in a gender opposite of their sex, or no gender at all?

The Bible's definition of love runs contrary to the Western world's definition. According to the world, loving someone means giving them license to pursue whatever they believe will bring them happiness or fulfillment. The Bible says that love requires truth. Love does not mean looking someone in the eyes and affirming every desire they experience. Love means looking someone in the eyes and communicating the truth of Scripture. We are to do so gently, but we are to do so nonetheless.

It is very important to bear in mind that what Christians call "loving" will not often be considered loving by the world. So we should never assess whether we are truly loving by the world's response to our message of love. Love and truth are never determined by whether they are popular—often, what is loving and true is very unpopular. Increasingly, speaking truth out of love is called "hate speech." But Paul says love cannot exist without truth and love cannot rejoice at wrongdoing. If we accept the authority of the Bible, we must understand that affirming people in a path that is contrary to what the Scripture teaches is never loving. If I affirm transgenderism, I am actually doing an unloving thing. I am withholding truth because I value my own reputation or my own friendships or my own comforts more than I value the eternal happiness of the person made in God's image who stands in front of me.

At the same time, speaking truth is not necessarily loving. There is a way of speaking biblical truth that is the opposite of loving—truth-speaking that is motivated by self-righteousness, pride, fear, or a desire to win an argument. It is loving to speak truth, but only if we speak truth lovingly:

> *A soft answer turns away wrath,*
> *but a harsh word stirs up anger. (Proverbs 15 v 1)*

No arrogance. No dismissal. No harsh words. No trite sayings that gloss over deeply personal experiences. No jokes, including those made behind someone's back.

Communicating truth and love requires relationship. If we really care about someone, we must tell them the truth. We have to love the truth so much that we care about truth more than we care about how the world thinks of us. We have to love people so much that we care about their souls more than we care about their approval. This means that the pursuit of truth and love may cost us friendships. People rejected Jesus for speaking the truth in love, and so we should expect the same.

LOVE PRODUCES COMPASSION

Put on then, as God's chosen ones, holy and beloved, compassionate hearts, kindness, humility, meekness, and patience. (Colossians 3 v 12)

If your experience is anything like mine, you might have first encountered the discussion around transgenderism with scoffing disbelief: "Ha! How absurd it is that people think they are a member of the opposite sex."

I am deeply, deeply sorry that I felt that way. It was wrong. It would hurt me if someone dismissed my feelings and my struggles as "absurd." I am sorry. I have needed to pray for forgiveness and for compassion.

A Christian's tendency is often to feel alarm at new ideas, especially when those ideas deny rather than support biblical truths. But compassion means we must disarm and deliberately lay down any negativity we have toward those who think or feel or live in that way—including those who experience gender dysphoria, or are seeking to become and live as the opposite gender to their birth sex, or to live with no gender at all.

After all, we claim the name of the sinless, divine, holy Son of God, who did not laugh at, mock or turn his nose up at all the great gamut of human sin that he encountered, for the first time in all eternity, during his time on earth. He met those who had rejected all his plans and desires for them not with fear or scorn but with compassion. Not only that—if you look at Jesus' stance toward "sinners," he was far more challenging to those who called themselves religious, thought of themselves as righteous, and looked down on others than he was of those who had deliberately chosen to follow a disobedient path. He called compassionately to the latter to return to the God they needed, even as those around him called him to reject them (have a read of Luke 5 v 29-32 and 7 v 36-50). Nowhere in the Gospels will you find Jesus pronouncing "woe" on anyone who is not the kind of proud, professing religious guy who looks down on others and thinks their views and decisions are absurd.

Compassion does not mean approval. But neither does compassion mean silence. Compassion says, "I'm so sorry you are experiencing deep inner anguish about your gender. I cannot fathom the types of struggles you experience, but I would like to listen to you and I would like to be here for you. I'm sorry for any hurt or rejection you've encountered from others. I want you to know that I am your friend and will walk with you through the valleys of your struggles. I want you to know that I may not agree with you, but I will never look down on you. You are loved."

LOVE HAS PATIENCE

Compassion means entering into someone else's pain with the confidence that the gentleness and kindness of God—and not the self-righteous, haughty correction of his people—is what leads to repentance:

> *Love is patient and kind; love does not envy or boast; it is not arrogant. (1 Corinthians 13 v 4)*

A believer who experiences gender dysphoria may never be freed of their gender dysphoria. Or maybe they will. The militant transgender activist who accuses those who disagree with pro-transgender ideology of bigotry or worse may never change their mind and place themselves under Christ's loving lordship. Or maybe they will.

That's the beauty of Christianity: we have a patient God. All too often, God's people act as if we believe that smugness, superiority, and angry moral pronouncements are what draws people to the gospel. In God's economy, kindness, forbearance, and patience are his instruments. God is rich in "kindness and forbearance and patience"— and "God's kindness is meant to lead you to repentance" (Romans 2 v 4).

Do you realize how patient God was with you, when you lived in deliberate rebellion against him? Do you realize how patient God still is with you, as you fail to love and obey his Son each day, despite knowing who he is and what he has done for you? No one should be more shocked that you have been born again than you. Though people's rebellion against God may differ in degree, it does not differ in type. Any rebellion is enough to separate us from God. And no rebellion is horrendous enough to put us out of the saving reach of God.

No one is more patient than our God; and if he is patient, so must we be, too.

We must be patient as we walk alongside those experiencing the anguish of gender dysphoria. We must be patient as we engage with those angry at the Christian gospel's good news about God's design for gender. We are not here to win arguments. We are here to love people.

It's so, so important to learn that the purpose of love, compassion, kindness and patience isn't simply to get a hearing in the culture, far less to make us popular in the culture. As Christians, we demonstrate these virtues not because they are methods for gaining popularity but because the Bible commends them as reflecting the character of God, and tells us that they are pleasing to God. We cannot ever be sure that our kindness and patience will win a hearing for the gospel. But we can always be certain that our self-righteousness and impatience will lose a hearing for the gospel.

FACE TO FACE

We live in the age of social media—and it is an age that is corrosive to loving our neighbor. Social media enables us to select our neighbors, and ignore everyone else. Facebook's algorithms mean that almost everyone we hear from via Facebook already agrees with our position (or is sharing a funny video). When our safe social-media bubbles are pierced by different views, it tends to be because something extreme has happened—and so we grow fearful as we see or hear how those who seek to love with truth are treated. Perhaps worst of all, we can pontificate without needing to listen or to see the effect of our reactions on those whose lives we are talking about.

Love requires relationship—real, face-to-face relationship. That's where we can learn how to love our neighbor.

Not so long ago, I and some Christian friends were involved in a prolonged and emotionally-fraught conversation with members of the LGBTQ community. It was a charged atmosphere. Prominent leaders and influence-formers from both sides were in the room. It looked like a set-up predisposed to conflict and civil war.

The evening began with a commitment to ground rules that could be summed up as "Respect." Everyone took turns discussing why they were in the room and why they had an interest in bridging the gap between the Christian and LGBTQ communities. While in the back of everyone's mind there was hope that people from both sides would change their mind, the biggest hope was to de-escalate some of the tensions that were engulfing the United States.

At one point a transgender woman (a biological man who self-identifies as a woman) stood up and pleaded, with great emotion, that all they wanted was to be able to go to the bathroom without fear of abuse or mockery in the restroom that aligned with their new identity.

While we were not persuaded by the bathroom argument being made, hearing the emotional plea of one person as they looked at us, face to face, helped us all understand that the person talking was not a bad person. They were not absurd. They were not intending harm. This was a human being made in God's image who thought God's blueprint was wrong. This person was not our enemy; this was a person to be embraced as a friend, listened to, and understood, even when (especially when) we disagreed.

There was no fighting that evening. No insults were thrown. Even when people disagreed, they did so charitably and without questioning the other person's motive.

No one expected one side to agree with the other or vice versa. We did hope that a discussion centered on controversial issues could proceed civilly and respectfully. And it did.

No one walked away from that evening convinced that the other side was right; but we did all walk away without feeling bitter or angry with one another. Dialogue happened. And though no side lessened their grip on their convictions, basic aspects of respect and extending dignity to one another allowed conversation and understanding to proceed.

This is just one example of what is required of every Christian. We are to love our neighbor. Every neighbor. Before we challenge another person about their life, we must challenge the person we see in the mirror about their love. Love does not mean we sacrifice truth on the altar of popularity. Love does not require sacrificing conviction. In fact, love demands that we don't. But love does mean deliberately, prayerfully and thoughtfully extending respect, empathy, compassion, and patience to everyone, equally, and indiscriminately.

In the past, I have failed to do this, in my thoughts if not in my words and actions. Many of us likely have failed in this way. For that sin, we need forgiveness, and in the gospel we have it. If we would claim the name of Christ, then we must live like him, and love like him.

9. NO EASY PATHS

What would it look like for someone to experience gender dysphoria and follow Jesus? What would it look like for someone who has had hormones and undergone gender-transitioning surgery to follow Jesus?

It would be very, very hard. And yet, at the same time, it would be experientially and eternally worthwhile.

I do not struggle with gender dysphoria. I never have. So I am sensitive to the accusation that anyone who does experience gender dysphoria may have reading this chapter: "How can Andrew give advice about gender dysphoria and my life when he has no idea what it feels like?" This is a good question, and it would be strange not to ask it.

My answer is that while in a very, very real sense someone with dysphoria experiences something radically different to anything that I do, in another very, very real sense they are experiencing something radically in common with me. I know the effects of brokenness in my life. And I know the experience of what feels right to me and what Jesus says is right for me—indeed, commands of me—sometimes being completely and painfully opposed.

This is the experience of what Jesus himself called cross-carrying.

A LIFE THAT IS HARDER (BUT NOT FOREVER)

Jesus told his disciples, "If anyone would come after me, let him deny himself and take up his cross and follow me. For whoever would save his life will lose it, but whoever loses his life for my sake will find it." (Matthew 16 v 24-25)

Jesus would not have made a great salesman. His lifestyle offer to us all runs totally contrary to the self-interest that motivates much of our decision-making. We usually buy into something based on the pleasure or happiness it brings up. But Jesus describes following him as taking up a cross—an ancient symbol for death, scorn, and rejection.

To carry a cross means to deny ourselves—to lose whatever defined and directed our lives before we met our Maker, came to him as our Savior and began to follow him as our Lord. The nature of that cross will be different from person to person. We may say the weight of that cross will be different for different people and at different times too. For some people, their cross is the loneliness of unwanted singleness. For others, their cross is stage 4 cancer eating away at vital organs. Others may experience searing depression that makes happiness a faraway island. Each of us has a cross. There are no easy paths following Christ. And if you are reading this as a Christian who cannot identify your cross—if, to be blunt, your life is characterized by comfort or compromise more than cross-carrying—then perhaps this chapter should stand as a challenge to you. You can never ask someone with gender dysphoria to shoulder their cross if you are not consciously carrying yours.

By definition, a cross is not something that you'd choose to carry for itself. Following Jesus makes life harder. As the seventeenth-century Scottish pastor Samuel Rutherford once wrote, "No man hath a velvet cross." So when it comes to gender dysphoria, Jesus is not promising that coming to him means walking away from that experience. He is asking someone to be willing to live with that dysphoria, perhaps for their whole lives—and to follow him nonetheless.

It may seem an unattractive sales pitch! But Jesus says that it's under the weight of the cross that we "find" life. We don't just take up our crosses and carry them without direction. We carry those crosses as we follow Jesus toward forever. And one day, as we saw in chapter seven, death will be past, our crosses will be laid down, and we'll enjoy eternity as the people we were designed to be. For the Christian, joy is eternal and hardship has an expiration date.

So what does it mean to follow Jesus while you experience gender dysphoria? It means your life will be very, very hard. The Christian life is hard—but not forever.

And there is more to say.

A LIFE THAT IS BETTER (NOW AS WELL AS FOREVER)

> *Peter said, "See, we have left our homes and followed you."*
> *And [Jesus] said to them, "Truly, I say to you, there is*
> *no one who has left house or wife or brothers or parents or*
> *children, for the sake of the kingdom of God, who will*
> *not receive many times more in this time, and in the age to*
> *come eternal life." (Luke 18 v 29-30)*

As we carry our crosses, Jesus says it is worth it. Jesus says that whoever embraces the life of costly discipleship will never be left to regret it. Jesus says that those who deny themselves and carry their cross to follow him will experience, now, a life of abundance—of more than just struggling; of more than just getting by; of more than just settling.

And here's part of what I think Jesus means: nothing in this life is without purpose and eternal reward if it is given to Jesus—even weakness and suffering.

The apostle Paul experienced great, ongoing pain. He does not tell us whether it was physical or psychological. But he does tell us that he repeatedly "pleaded" with Jesus to take it away. And he does tell us that Jesus answered:

> *"My grace is sufficient for you, for my power is made perfect in weakness."*
> *Therefore [Paul says] I will boast all the more gladly of my weaknesses, so that the power of Christ may rest upon me. For the sake of Christ, then, I am content with weaknesses, insults, hardships, persecutions, and calamities. For when I am weak, then I am strong.*
> *(2 Corinthians 12 v 9-10)*

It is often in times of pain that we discover how powerful God is; how full of kindness he is; how strong he is able to make us even when in ourselves we are only weak.

A few years ago, my wife had a miscarriage. It was fairly late for first-trimester miscarriages and it came after a period of time when it had been hard to get pregnant. The pain I felt at the moment we were told that no heartbeat had been detected on the sonogram was soul-crushing. This was the first time I had truly grieved as an adult, and it was the first time that my wife and I grieved together.

But as I reflect back on that time, what I always remember was the sense of calm I had as I cried out to God. In that sense of grief, I never felt abandoned. In fact, just the opposite occurred—in my grief—in our grief—I discovered that God's grace was more than sufficient.

God's kindness showed itself in a hundred little ways, his grace reflecting to me through the grace he inspired in others. I recall our old church community reaching out to me from hundreds of miles away to console us. I recall our new church immediately coming to our support. I recall a friend—who I don't always agree with on theological and political issues—contacting me and offering me his parents' vacation house if we wanted to use it just to get away.

The pain is a cross I will bear. I would never have chosen it, and would never choose it for anyone. But I never felt closer to God than I did at that time. I never experienced power and grace and strength from outside of me—from outside of this world—as I did at that time. It is better to carry a cross behind Jesus if bearing it brings you close to the one who carried his own cross for you.

I know that everyone's story of suffering is going to be different. I know the circumstances of what causes people to suffer are going to be different. I know your struggle may far, far outstrip mine. But what I know from Jesus' promise and my own experience is this: suffering and experiencing hardship, when borne as a cross as you follow Jesus, is never without purpose and can never extinguish your hope.

I've never met someone who was a Christian that didn't find immense comfort from God in the midst of suffering. Every joyful Christian I've met who's suffered has always believed they were better off somehow for having experienced affliction.

Dr. Mark Yarhouse has written a helpful book from a Christian perspective on understanding gender dysphoria. I don't agree with all of Dr. Yarhouse's advice and counsel (especially on the question of how to cope with experiencing gender dysphoria as a follower of Jesus), but much of what is in his book is very, very helpful.

On the question of what it means for those with gender dysphoria to experience suffering, Dr. Yarhouse puts it wonderfully well:

> *"It should not be assumed that greater Christlikeness is the same as having experiences of gender dysphoria abate. Rather, many people who know and love Christ have besetting conditions that have simply not resolved as a result of their belief in Christ as their Savior. Indeed, it may very well be that it is in the context of these enduring conditions that God brings about greater Christlikeness."* [21]

Dr. Yarhouse's book includes a beautiful quote from Melinda Selmys (a woman whom I have had the privilege to meet and spend time with). Selmys struggles with gender dysphoria. Her view is well worth quoting in full:

> *"Suffering in Christianity is not only not meaningless, it is ultimately one of the most powerful media for the transmission of meaning. We can stand in adoration between [sic] the cross, and kneel and kiss the wood that bore the body of our Savior, because this is the means by which the ugly meaningless atheistic suffering of the world (the problem of evil) was transmuted into the living water, the blood of Christ, the wellspring of Creation. The great paradox here is that the Tree of Death and Suffering is the Tree of Life. This central paradox in Christianity allows us to love our own brokenness precisely because it is through that brokenness that we image the broken body of our God—and the highest expression of divine love. That God in some sense wills it to be so seems evident*

---

21 *Understanding Gender Dysphoria:*, page 148.

*in Gethsemane: Christ prays, 'Not my will, but thine be
done,' and when God's will is done it involves the scourge
and the nails. It's also always struck me as particularly
fitting and beautiful that when Christ is resurrected his
body is not returned to a state of perfection, as the body
of Adam in Eden, but rather it still bears the marks of
his suffering and death.* "[22]

The Christian life is a life of cross-carrying. Gender
dysphoria is the cross that some are called to bear. To
choose to follow Christ and carry that cross makes life
harder, but not forever. And it means life is better, now
as well as eternally.

OK, BUT WHAT WILL IT LOOK LIKE?

We need to return to the questions with which we began
this chapter: what does cross-carrying discipleship mean
for someone who experiences gender dysphoria, or who
has fully embraced a transgender identity?

Imagine that your neighbor, Alexandra, whom you've
befriended since she moved onto your street three years
ago and who hasn't been inside a church building since
she was a child, has come to your church for eight weeks
in a row.

At first, Alex (as she likes to be known) seemed to fit
right in and really enjoy it. You were excited! But over the
last three Sundays, you've noticed that after the service,
she's left quickly, looking visibly shaken. You're worried,
but haven't found the right moment to ask her what exactly is wrong.

Finally, one Tuesday night, Alex shows up at your door.
Her eyes are red and puffy from crying.

---

22 Quoted in *Understanding Gender Dysphoria*, pages 59-60.

You invite her in, and ask her what is wrong.

Over the dinner table and coffee, she musters up the energy to tell you, "I want to repent of my sin and follow Jesus."

Overjoyed, you smile happily at Alex. But something seems strange. You're joyful. She is not.

You talk some more. It's clear that she understands the gospel—and as she's explaining who she knows Jesus is and what it means to become a Christian, she obsessively fixates on the word "repentance." She repeats it, stammering. And then she loses it, sobbing.

Shoulders downward and in a tone of anguish and terror, Alex fills you in on her story. Alex tells you that she was born a "he"—Alexander. From an early age, Alex felt like a woman trapped in a man's body. At 19, suffering with depression and exhausted from feeling "different," Alex started to "transition"—at first taking hormones, then making the decision to change name to "Alexandra," and finally, at 25, having gender reassignment surgery. From all appearances—physique, voice, and even anatomy—Alex looks like a woman.

And for over 25 years, Alex has lived as Alexandra. Because she has moved from suburban Chicago to Atlanta, Alex's community, her friends and her employer all know her as a woman.

After recounting her story, Alex says to you, her only Christian friend, "I think Jesus says that what I have done is wrong. I feel for the first time in 25 years that maybe I was wrong. I think perhaps Jesus made me to be Alexander—a 'he.' And I want to follow Jesus—but I am afraid of what that will look like for me."

You may think you will never be in this situation. But pray that you will be—because, as we've seen, those in Alex's situation will only find what they are searching for in the gospel. The next chapter will focus on the response of the church to individuals like Alex; but for now, the question is: what should be the repentant response to Jesus of Alex and people in this position? What will it look like for Alex to follow Jesus?

- Must "she" revert back to a "he"? Should Alex ask people to speak to and about Alex as a "he"?[23] And if so, does this have to begin immediately?
- Does Alex stop the hormones?
- Does Alex have surgery to reverse the appearance of being a female?
- Does repentance mean Alex forsaking community and relationships?
- Must Alex no longer have feelings of gender dysphoria?

BLACK AND WHITE AND GRAY

There are answers to the above questions, but the solutions are not simple. They're complex, and awkward. Sometimes they are in shades of gray, not black and white.

First and foremost, as we've seen, Alex is going to have to be prepared to deny his feelings and preferences, even his identity of the last 25 years, in the here and now. Following Jesus will mean he picks up his cross, and trusts Jesus when he says that Alex will find true life only in him and on his terms. That promise is not conditional; otherwise, it wouldn't be a promise. The first step in discipleship for Alex is to come to grips with the call of discipleship: to obey Jesus—even when it runs contrary to strong inner desires.

With Alex, we must patiently, compassionately, and lovingly plead for him to see his created anatomical biology

---

23 I discuss pronoun usage for people in Alex's position on page 157.

as the God-given evidence of who he is. He is Alexander. None of this promises to be immediate or easy. And a costly walk of discipleship will likely encounter slip-ups along the way, and those stumbles do not indicate a lack of saving faith any more than my own stumbles do. As the theologian and ethicist Russell Moore has written about someone in Alexander's position, honesty is going to be a key issue in starting life as a disciple:

> *"He should present himself as what he is, a man created by God as such. This means he should identify himself as a man, and should start dressing in male clothing. This is going to be very, very difficult for him, and he will need his pastors and congregation to bear with him through all the stumbles and backsteps that will come along with this."*[24]

How a person begins to accept and live out their biological sex and God-given gender is going to look different for different individuals. For some, there may be instantaneous acceptance. For others, it may be long and painful, and involve as many troughs as peaks. Accepting God's authority over our lives is easier than coming to grips with all the implications of that in our lives. What matters is the attitude of repentance—of Christ being ruler, not self. Actions will, sooner or later, flow from that.

I think there is room for debate and discussion about how soon actions like this should be expected. It is arbitrary to suggest that someone in Alexander's position needs to be restored to full masculine appearance and self-identity from day one. What matters, I think, is whether there are intentional efforts to work toward reversing the effects of taking on a transgender identity.

---

24 "Joan or John? An Ethical Dilemma," *The Southern Baptist Journal of Theology 13*, no. 2 (Summer 2009), page 54.

Alex "becoming" (or, rather, reverting to living as) a man instantaneously is less important than seeing himself as a new creation in Christ instantaneously.

So, in Alexander's particular situation, this is going to mean, over time, returning to his original name. Hormonal therapy should begin to decrease to the point of stopping. But then there is the question of whether someone who has had gender-reassignment surgery should undergo additional surgery to revert. Personally, I don't think repentance demands this. The truth is that Alexander's first operation never really changed his sex or gender—it just surgically altered his bodily appearance. Even while identifying as Alexandra, he was still a male. As Russell Moore writes:

> *"There is no way that this surgery can be 'reversed,' only another illusion created on top of the old one."* [25]

Having said that, I don't think it is wrong if Alexander has surgery to restore him as closely as possible to his original male physiology. I think it is an option for a disciple; but I don't think it is an obligation for a disciple.

What matters is that, hard though it will be, Alexander accepts that his God-given sex and gender are now to direct his decisions and the way that he seeks to see himself. Hard though it will be, Jesus is calling him to rely on his Spirit to enable him to cope with his gender dysphoria, rather than to look to a different wardrobe, new hormones or invasive surgery to help him.

IT IS MEANINGFUL

Perhaps you are in Alex's position, reading this book because you have come to realize that Jesus offers you everything

---

25 As previous.

you need, for this life and the next—but coming to terms with what that might mean for the lifestyle you have adopted and the decisions you have made. Perhaps you are Alex's friend, and unsure of what to say and how to counsel your friend.

I don't want to sound as if I don't have some appreciation of what I am saying to you or to your friend, and how hard it will be. I am not unaware of the cost you are being called to. But I do want to say that Jesus does not offer a half-discipleship option. He asks you to give him everything, because he died to give you far more back. And he promises that he can use your struggles with your gender identity to show you his love, power, and strength. He can give it all purpose.

I am reminded of a beautiful section of a song by Shane and Shane, *Though You Slay Me,* that quotes from this portion of a sermon by the pastor John Piper:

> *"Not only is all your affliction momentary, not only is all your affliction light in comparison to eternity and the glory there. But all of it is totally meaningful. Every millisecond of your pain, from the fallen nature or fallen man, every millisecond of your misery in the path of obedience is producing a peculiar glory you will get because of that … It wasn't meaningless. It's doing something! It's not meaningless … It's not. It's working for you an eternal weight of glory.*
>
> *"Therefore, therefore, do not lose heart. But take these truths and day by day focus on them. Preach them to yourself every morning. Get alone with God and preach his word into your mind until your heart sings with confidence that you are new and cared for."* [26]

---

26 www.desiringgod.org/articles/a-song-for-the-suffering-with-john-piper.

If you are reading this as a Christian who is struggling with gender dysphoria, don't give up. If you are led to despair, don't give up. Ask a Christian you trust for help. Ask the Lord who mounted a cross for you for help. Your life is precious, wonderful and beautiful. You were made by God for God. And one day, your cross-carrying days will be over and you will be with God. Hear Jesus promise you this:

> *I say to you, there is no one who has left the gender identity that they felt more comfortable with, or the community they identified with, or the life they had expected and dreamed of, for the sake of the kingdom of God, who will not receive many times more—identity and community and life— in this time, and in the age to come eternal life.*

10. CHALLENGING THE CHURCH

A church should be the safest place to talk about, be open about, and struggle with gender dysphoria.

That is because the place where Jesus expects people to experience the truth of his promises is in his community— the church.

> *Peter began to say to him, "See, we have left everything*
> *and followed you." Jesus said, "Truly, I say to you, there*
> *is no one who has left house or brothers or sisters or mother*
> *or father or children or lands, for my sake and for the*
> *gospel, who will not receive a hundredfold now in this time,*
> *houses and brothers and sisters and mothers and children*
> *and lands, with persecutions, and in the age to come eternal*
> *life." (Mark 10 v 28-30)*

Peter says, "We have left everything." Peter and the disciples were following Jesus *together*. And this "we" had left everything. In response, Jesus promises that it is this "we" that will gain the rewards of an eternal hope—and not just this, but also that right now anyone who has given up precious hopes, relationships or securities for his sake will find far more in following him. Crucially, the place where he envisages people receiving a hundred times more in terms of open homes and loving family must be, and can only be... *in the church*.

"We" is one of the most important words in the Christian vocabulary for shaping our identity as Christians, and often we overlook the way that walking behind Christ requires fellowship with one another. We bear our crosses together in community, and community is what makes cross-bearing possible.

So a transgender person ought to feel more loved and safe visiting a Bible-believing church than in any other place in the world! A gender-dysphoric person should feel safer speaking about their identity and struggles in church than anywhere else—because they're loved in church. Church should be the place where people know they are loved, even if they disagree.

Too often, our churches have been anything but those places—and that is something that Christians, including me, need to say sorry for. If you're struggling with gender dysphoria and have found church unwelcoming, distant, judgmental or harsh when you have sought to open up, then there is a huge problem—and it's not yours; it's the church's. And I'm sorry.

Last chapter, we looked at Jesus' call to individuals. This chapter looks at the Bible's challenge to church communities who want to be the people Jesus wants them to be—and who therefore wish to embrace gender-dysphoric members, and reach out to gender-dysphoric and transgender neighbors, with love, loving truth, and truth-based hope.

What will that kind of church community be like?

COMPASSIONATE COMMUNITIES

If a popular local politician and also a self-identified transgender individual walked into your church, who would be
greeted first?

Who would the church's welcome team be more pleased
to see, and go the extra mile to make sure they felt at
home?

Who would be invited back the following Sunday?

If your honest answer is that the politician would be
the highest priority and receive the warmest welcome, the
hard truth is that the Bible says that your church would be
showing partiality—which is a sin:

> *My brothers, show no partiality as you hold the faith in
> our Lord Jesus Christ, the Lord of glory. For if a man
> wearing a gold ring and fine clothing comes into your
> assembly, and a poor man in shabby clothing also comes
> in, and if you pay attention to the one who wears the fine
> clothing and say, "You sit here in a good place," while you
> say to the poor man, "You stand over there," or, "Sit down
> at my feet," have you not then made distinctions among
> yourselves and become judges with evil thoughts? Listen,
> my beloved brothers, has not God chosen those who are
> poor in the world to be rich in faith and heirs of the king-
> dom, which he has promised to those who love him?*
>
> *(James 2 v 1-5)*

The church's response to those who identify as transgender, and to those who struggle with gender dysphoria but
who are not actively identifying as transgender, must be—
immediately and with integrity, "You are welcome here.
You are loved here."

Christians, this requires us to be open about our own
struggles and failings and worries. Too often our churches

give the impression that the Son of Man came to seek and save good people, not the lost. Too quickly our churches create a list of sins that are more tolerated and excusable (these tend to be the ones we struggle with) than others (which, conveniently, tend to be those that others struggle with).

The antidote to this is to understand that the compassion we need for others begins with appreciating the compassion that the Lord extends to each of us. He is the Lord of glory (James 2 v 1)—yet he came with words of welcome to those who had run from him. He is the Lord of glory—yet he loves and cares for you and me. That is the compassion we must be willing to extend to others—all others.

LISTENING COMMUNITIES

Know this, my beloved brothers: let every person be quick to hear, slow to speak, slow to anger. (James 1 v 19)

Blog threads, sermons, and post-church interactions can bend toward the reverse of this, particularly when it comes to hot-button issues. I know that's true of me! We feel angry, so we speak quickly, and we don't really want to listen at all.

Very often, churches who are committed to the Bible as God's word, and who honestly want to love others as Christ loves them, fail to listen. Why? Because we know we have our theology perfectly zipped up and our apologetics perfectly charted, so we think we need simply to expound truths that heads in the pews will absorb. The problem, though, is that God made us with both heads and hearts: with thoughts, feelings, and desires. In order to impact someone's heart, we need to listen to their hearts too.

Real people live in our neighborhoods, sit in our church

buildings, and talk with us after our services, and they have real struggles. And the question is: in our churches, do they hear their struggles spoken about kindly, carefully, by someone who has tried to understand them? Or quickly, dismissively, and angrily, by someone who has never stopped to think how they feel? Would someone secretly struggling with gender dysphoria hear it talked about in a way that invites them to open up, or which tells them never, ever to risk it—in a way that assumes "people like that" are not sitting in church that Sunday, or that recognizes they may well be?

When it comes to gender identity, we need to listen to what it's like to struggle in this area. And we need to be willing to hear hard truths about how we in the church have—either through lack of thought, or lack of love, or just with the best of intentions—hurt people who encounter gender-identity issues.

We need to listen to the person in front of us, rather than assuming they conform to a stereotype in our head which is likely based on media stories, or social-media gossip. It's annoying when folks outside the church assume that all Christians are members of extreme, hatred-fueled groups such as Westboro Baptist Church, and it's no less rude when we fail to listen to someone because we have already decided what they are like, and what they want.

The twentieth-century German theologian and martyr Dietrich Bonhoeffer rightly observed:

> *"The first service that one owes to others in the fellowship consists of listening to them. Just as love of God begins with listening to his word, so the beginning of love for our brothers and sisters is learning to listen to them."* [27]

---

27 *Life Together* (Fortress Press, 1995), page 98.

There are no exceptions to this truth. And there are no Christians who do not need to contribute to making sure that the message from their church community can honestly be, "Come to the church and be heard."

If you don't know much about gender-identity issues and don't know what it is like to struggle with them, learn to listen. Take time to listen. Be ready to learn. If someone says, "You don't understand," then rather than telling them they're wrong, answer, "Very possibly not. Please tell me."

Listening opens us up to hearing that we've got something wrong. And that's OK. It's unlikely that we have got our theology 100% correct. It's certain we haven't got our thinking and behavior 100% correct. Humility dictates that we are willing to acknowledge we have been wrong.

Paul urges the church in Ephesus to...

> *... walk in a manner worthy of the calling to which you have been called. (Ephesians 4 v 1)*

What does that look like? Interacting with others...

> *... with all humility and gentleness, with patience, bearing with one another in love, eager to maintain the unity of the Spirit in the bond of peace. (v 2-3)*

According to Paul, we walk consistent with what our Lord calls us to when we live with humility, gentleness, and patience. This means that failing to display these virtues to our brothers and sisters who struggle with dysphoria is to disobey what the gospel has called us to.

We in the local church ought to be willing to accept weaknesses, admit ignorance, recognize complexity, wrestle with real life, and change where necessary. This does not mean that we weaken our convictions (as I'll write below). But it does mean being a church humble enough to know that while it has in the gospel the answers for every person's greatest problem (sin and brokenness), speaking well into very real lives with very real problems requires a willingness to listen well before we speak lovingly.

CONVICTIONAL COMMUNITIES

Think about other communities with a cause. The cause may not be noble—in fact, it may be ignoble, stoking racism, promoting greed, or justifying casual sex—but if a group has a cause, its members do not lack confidence in their convictions as they contend for people's attention and hearts.

How sad it would be for the people of God to not have full confidence in our cause. How sad it would be if the people of God lost the conviction that relationship with the God who has revealed himself in the Bible is what each inhabitant of this world was made for.

Jesus says that to trust him is to understand truth and experience freedom:

> *If you abide in my word, you are truly my disciples, and*
> *you will know the truth, and the truth will set you free.*
> *(John 8 v 31-32)*

Because the middle part of this book was about understanding and grappling with the truth of Scripture when it comes to the question of gender identity, we do not need to repeat that here. But we do need to underline that if a church community is to be a lifeline of hope to those who struggle with gender dysphoria, it must be one committed to biblical truth. Why? Not because it feels good to be right, but because it allows us to offer a word of hope and reconciliation. We can only offer this message if we believe the message is true!

If Christians have anything to offer in this contentious age, it is truth, and we should not shy away from that truth. But equally, if we use truth as blunt force trauma against those who are coming to grips with what discipleship means, woe to us. Woe to us if we demand conformity from those who are struggling more than we are willing to walking alongside them while they are struggling.

It is only loving to hold to biblical truth if that truth comes wrapped in love. We are only firmly anchored, able to grow and to share the gospel without being tossed about by every idea and argument from both the conservative and progressive ends of the spectrum, if we are "speaking the truth in love" (Ephesians 4 v 15). Neither love nor truth is an optional bolt-on to our Christianity.

Most of us, depending on our particular character, tend to bend toward one or the other: to love or to truth. The struggle is to showcase the one we bend away from.

If you or your church tends to listen and love but bend the truth in your attempt to love, the challenge is: hold to the truth, even as you love—remember that loving someone is not the same as agreeing with them, and sometimes loving someone requires you to disagree. But for those of us who are tempted to teach truth without love, the challenge is: don't neglect love. After all, it's love that wins a hearing for the truth that inspired that love in the first place.

STEADFAST COMMUNITIES

You may know Paul as the man who brought the gospel to city after city around the Mediterranean. But the gospel was not all he was committed to sharing with those he met:

*We were gentle among you, like a nursing mother taking
care of her own children. So, being affectionately desirous
of you, we were ready to share with you not only the gospel
of God but also our own selves, because you had become
very dear to us. (1 Thessalonians 2 v 7-8)*

If someone struggles with gender dysphoria, then life will
be hard if they follow Christ, and there will be ups and
downs (as we saw in the last chapter). We need to love
one another for the long haul and through the hard times.
Love means sharing life with people and making ourselves
vulnerable to hurt and heartbreak. This means embracing
the annoyances and the interruptions that come with being
a friend. Lots of us want to be friends in the abstract, but
when it comes time to display radical commitment to a
friend, we'd rather be left unbothered.

Notice the image that Paul invokes. His ministry
was one of vulnerable gentleness. Like a mother who
cares for her children, and whose heart is wrapped up
with their fortunes... that is how Christians are to see
the other members of their churches. To be the church
means to work hard and spend much in the pursuit of
being a community that walks through the mountains and
the valleys together—including with those whose struggles are unlike our own.

How do we do this? Gently. Gentleness is the opposite
of harshness. Gentleness is a tender voice and an arm
around the shoulder; it is not a stern lecture with a point-
ed finger in someone's chest. Gentleness refuses to judge
others condemningly. We can know what gentleness is by
how we wish others would act toward us when we are burdened by a weakness or crushed by a sin (ours or another's). Let us not only be gospel-sharing communities, but
self-sharing communities.

GRACIOUS COMMUNITIES

It's very easy to miss, but Paul's letters to the churches he ministered to always begin and finish, one way or another, with the word "grace." That's because grace, God's overwhelming kindness, is the first word and the last word of Christian hope, Christian community, and Christian life.

Local churches should point to God's grace all the time—holding to our Creator's standards because we know they are for the good of his creatures, but also celebrating his overwhelming forgiveness and extending our own forgiveness.

What does grace tell me? It tells me that I fall short, and so do you. Grace tells me I am still loved, and so are you. Grace is there for me in my repentance, and it's there for you in yours. Grace says forgiveness is always available—for me, and for you.

I need grace desperately, and so do you. We all need it in equal amounts, because it's the oxygen we breathe to sustain the Christian life.

Grace says there is no one outside the reach of God, including you and including me:

> *For by grace you have been saved through faith. And this is not your own doing; it is the gift of God, not a result of works, so that no one may boast. For we are his workmanship, created in Christ Jesus for good works, which God prepared beforehand, that we should walk in them.*
>
> *(Ephesians 2 v 8-10)*

From start to finish, salvation belongs to Jesus—and the grace that first saved us is the grace that works in us to make us more like Jesus. Grace never lets us be proud, for our salvation is not of our own doing; but grace also prevents us from despair, for by grace we have been saved and are being remade.

If our churches are marked by one thing, let it be grace—the grace that always welcomes in, always goes the extra mile, always forgives, and never says "enough."

BE THE CHURCH THAT YOU (AND EVERYONE ELSE) NEED

The way of Jesus involves carrying a cross, but it also offers a compassionate community. How wonderfully odd it is to consider that Jesus saves us not by removing us or our challenges from this world, but by giving us the strength to face those challenges together.

Your church is to be a place of grace, a place where everyone, no matter what their background or struggles are, finds homes open and family offered; a place where the door is always open rather than the drawbridge drawn up; a place where people are listened to and loved rather than stereotyped and lectured at. If you are a church member—whether you're a senior pastor, an elder, a young teenager, or a new Christian—you are called to serve that end.[28]

That makes your church harder and costlier to be a part of. That will involve you being willing to be challenged and to be changed, and resisting the temptation always to assume that it's only others who get things wrong.

But that also makes your church the church that you need, and that those around you need—and the church that pleases your Lord, as you live with grace while you speak of grace.

---

28 For more on being this kind of Christian community, go to harvestusa.org.

11. SPEAKING TO CHILDREN

"Today at school, while my ten-year-old son was in the restroom, a girl his age came in and used the restroom. Except he says she's not a girl anymore—now she's called Bryce.

"I know the bathroom controversies may seem insignificant. But until it is your kid who is having to deal with the change in culture, you never realize how challenging this topic is. And I'm struggling. My son and I went on an hour-long walk tonight to talk about it. I never thought I would have to explain to my son what transgenderism is at such a young age."

This was a text exchange between a good Christian friend and me not so long ago. You may have had a similar experience to my friend. Maybe you've gone for a walk to talk about it with your child. Or, perhaps your experience is that your daughter or your son has told you that they feel like Bryce does.

And the question is: on that hour-long walk, what do you say?

MOM AND DAD, CAN YOU EXPLAIN TO ME?

If you are a parent, it is going to be impossible to avoid this topic. It's not a question of if you'll have to talk to your son or daughter about the growing acceptance of transgenderism; it's a matter of when. When that happens, what will you say?

Will you shrug your shoulders in disbelief and avoid the topic altogether, leaving your child to be informed and have their opinions shaped only by the outside world?

Will you respond in mocking disbelief, and tell your kids, "Those people are crazy. They just need to know what it means to be a man or a woman. And that'll take care of it."

Will you panic, withdraw your child from school, and aim to shield them from this—and everything else that is wrong "out there" in the world?

Or will you sit down and have a difficult and honest conversation about a challenging topic that their young minds may find very difficult to understand?

You can't avoid your child having this conversation, sooner or later. The question is whether your child will have it with you, or with someone else. If you find yourself wanting to avoid the topic altogether, and your child knows it, not only will it communicate that you don't want to help your child navigate challenging topics; it will suggest to them that Christians lack the ability to give a compassionate, nuanced answer, and that your faith can't cope with reality.

The temptation to shield our children from such topics is understandable, but it is not acceptable. A part of being wise as a parent is balancing a desire to protect your child from the world with the need to prepare them for the world. So what you say to your eight-year-old is going to look different than what you would tell your sixteen-year-old. But you're going to have to say something.

So here's what I'd say to a ten-year-old on an hour-long walk:

- People see reality in different ways, and Christians base our view of reality on what the Bible teaches about the world, because it is written by the God who made us.

- God made men and women equally valuable, and he made them to be different, and this difference is wonderful and good, and is what leads to humans reproducing in every generation. The human race relies on sexual difference. I'd talk, in an age-appropriate way, about the unique traits of being a boy, and being a girl.

- I'd also aim to poke holes in cultural stereotypes about gender. I'd tell my child that not every man likes to hunt or watch football. Some men enjoy cooking and writing poetry. Not every young girl wants to wear princess dresses. Some girls may enjoy tramping through the woods in overalls. And that's okay. Not all men are going to act like men in the same way that the culture demands. Not all women are going to act like women in the same way that the culture demands. And that's okay. I'd point out to them that in our church, there are men who are sports-obsessed, unlike their dad! Equally, there are men who can't fix a car, like their dad! And there are women who don't enjoy cooking, and women who run their own business, and women who love cooking and work in the home.

- While God made a very good world, it's been messed up by sin, and sin causes brokenness in the world and, in very different ways, in people's lives. I would be looking to make very clear that there is a difference between suffering the effects of a sinful world, and active personal sin; and that we are all sinners, including them, in different ways. (You'll notice I'm basically taking my child on a walking tour of Genesis 1 – 3.)

• The biblical view of this world is not one that everyone shares. People who reject God's good rule are not going to accept God's teaching. Sometimes, we don't feel like accepting it either.

• Some people feel they were born a different gender than their birth sex and they feel alienated from their body. Feeling like this really upsets them, and it's a very hard place to be in. We don't need to be mean to these people, and we must never consider them weird or freakish because they're made by God, in his image. But we need to remember that God made them to be a man or a woman, with a male body or a female body, and so how they feel about themselves is not what God wants for them. Bryce is a girl, because God made her that way.

• In a fallen world, every human is walking with sin and brokenness that they did not choose and that they cannot simply walk away from. And so every Christian sometimes has to say "no" to what they want or how they feel, because Jesus is their King. To be a Christian means we trust in God even when it seems different than what our experiences, perceptions, and desires say. To be a Christian also means loving those around us, even when—perhaps especially when—we disagree with them. That's what Jesus did.

If your child asks a question you don't have an answer to, have the courage to say, "I don't know. But let me do some studying about what the Bible says about that." Being honest with your children about hard topics, and letting them know you are committed to helping them instead of giving them some ham-fisted answer, will demonstrate that you are serious about helping them navigate a challenging culture thoughtfully.

Finally, find ways to keep this conversation going. Naturally, as your child grows, it will. As a child matures and experiences new phases of life, there are going to be natural questions about proper expectations and how that child understands himself or herself as a man or as a woman. Encourage that. Don't run away from important questions about sexual and gender identity just because your pre-pubescent child, or pubescent teen, is asking hard and awkward questions. Reject the temptation to offload parental responsibility in the awkwardness of puberty. That's when your child needs your greatest attention, your confidence, and your affirmation. In the home as much as in the church, we each bend toward harsh "truth" or untruthful "love"—and we need to be aware of this in our parenting. We need to pray about, and against, whatever particular tendency we as parents might have when parenting our kids.

Communicate confidently, but not arrogantly. Communicate compassionately, not harshly. Communicate honestly, not simplistically or tritely.

MOM AND DAD, CAN YOU HELP ME?

"Mom and Dad, I know a lot about what it means to be transgender because of what I see on television. I'm scared, confused, and I do not know how you will respond, but I want you to know that for a long time, I've felt very different and uncomfortable in my body. When I've tried to pinpoint how it is I feel, I feel more like a boy than a girl. I think I'm transgender."

Maybe this has happened to you already and this is why you have purchased this book. Or maybe some day this will happen and you want to be prepared in advance.

What do you say in this moment? How do you react?

It matters. These few seconds are perhaps some of the most consequential of your child's life, and of yours.

Whether your child encounters an embrace born of love or scowling eyebrows can make all the difference to their future, and to your future as your child's parent. So the first thing to say has to be, "I love you. I am your mom/dad, and I love you, and I always will." Express unflinching devotion to your child. Never for a moment should your child question your commitment to them.

Second, invite your child to talk about how they are feeling and what they are thinking, in full. Don't interrupt; don't try to process their feelings for them, far less correct their thinking—just listen. Just listen.

Third, remember their age. I know that sounds strange—most of us can remember the age of our own kids! But your response will be different based on your child's stage in life, as well as on whether your child is fully identifying as transgender, or is speaking of his or her experiences with gender dysphoria, or is wondering whether they should think of themselves as the opposite gender (or none).

So for a four-year-old, we should not read too much into things if a young child says they'd like to be the opposite gender. They're likely testing the bounds of what is possible in order to explore and think through the world they're living in (similar to how kids sometimes say, "I think I will be the mommy/daddy today"). With young children, don't panic. Don't worry if a boy wants to play with dolls. It almost certainly doesn't mean anything! Don't panic if a girl says she wants to be a boy. It likely just means she wants to do things that boys she knows do.

For an eight-year-old, then, this may be different, if the feelings are persistent—but here it's crucial to remember that, even if a pre-pubescent child really does feel they are the opposite gender, statistically the vast majority of individuals outgrow these feelings.[29] This is why the phenomenon of children being given medical intervention that blocks hormones during puberty is so troubling, because those hormones are an important component of our gender matching our sex. Puberty almost always enables children who feel some sense of gender dysphoria to grow, we might say, into their biological sex.

For a teenager, this conversation is going to be different, and harder. One thing worth saying is that how you feel is not necessarily who you are. This runs totally contrary to the Western world's wisdom, and so it needs gently saying, and gently repeating. If your child is professing faith, it is also worth underlining what we looked at in chapter nine—that the Christian life of discipleship is about carrying a cross, and that this may be an aspect of their cross-carrying, for a season or for a longer time. Pray with them, asking the Lord to help them work through their feelings honestly, and humbly, and wisely and obediently.

Fourth, contact your local church and let a team of pastors know what is happening in your family's life. It is absolutely crucial that a parent or a child doesn't hide themselves for fear of embarrassment at how they will be perceived in their church.

Fifth, assess the needs of your child emotionally and psychologically. Because our culture is so fraught with politicized perspectives on treatment for someone who

---

29 Lawrence S. Mayer, Paul R. McHugh, Executive Summary, "Sexuality and Gender: Findings from the Biological, Psychosocial, and Social Sciences," *The New Atlantis,* www.thenewatlantis.com/publications/executive-summary-sexuality-and-gender.

experiences gender dysphoria, I would counsel you to search for a Christian counselor or psychologist who is a trained expert in mental health, but who also refuses to embrace all the ideological underpinnings that come with transgenderism. This is not a book on treating someone who experiences gender-identity confusion—you may well need to find a Christian expert who can help with that.

If I can emphasize one particular point of counsel, it is this: let your pastor or church's elders know of your situation. Let them be the pastors and shepherds that God has called them to be. Do not fear; reject embarrassment. Run into the arms of your local church.

A LOST CHILD IS A PRODIGAL SON

I've heard of stories about young adults who are transgender and from Christian homes who have been cut off by their parents and told they are not welcome at home or at the dinner table.

This is wrong.

A child who rejects your faith and rebels against their Creator will never cease to be your child. And a rebellious child who you reject is extremely unlikely ever to cease to rebel.

Let me be as exceedingly and abundantly clear on this as I have been on anything else in this book: *There is no justification for abandoning your child—ever.* Abandoning your child because he or she rejects your faith's teaching is just as bad as your child abandoning his or her birth sex. Your call to be a parent is not conditional upon whether your child agrees with you, believes what you do, or lives as you do.

A few years back, I took a phone call from a Christian whose son had run away to a big city in order to be in a homosexual relationship. The son had abandoned his Christian faith. Obviously, the father was distraught. I quickly noticed that while the father obviously disagreed with his son's homosexuality, he was more heartsick at his son's absence. That was very telling in the moment, because it communicated something about parenthood: a parent's love is meant to be enduring. This dad told me that his son would not agree to meet with him unless he would meet both him and his boyfriend together.

He asked what I would do. I told him that I did not see in Scripture any evidence that a rebellious son's disobedience nullified the boy's sonship. Nor did it nullify this man's identity and role as a father. I told him that if he wanted to see his son, that if he had any hopes of his son repenting in the future, what mattered right now was communicating unconditional love to his son. I told him that, if it were me, I would drive to the city where his son was and meet with him as soon as possible. I was not asking him to agree with his son. I was not asking him to abandon biblical teaching. I was asking him not to abandon his child in his actions, just as his lovesick voice over the phone was showing he had not done in his heart.

Whatever self-righteous attempt at saving face has infected Christianity with the idea that a child's disobedience nullifies a parent's love for a child and a relationship with a child—this must end right now. If you are a parent who has consigned your child to a life apart from you because he or she is identifying as the opposite sex, please repent. Their sin doesn't justify yours. This does not mean that your child wants to be at your home, but it is absolutely vital that you make clear that you want that.

After all, we have all been prodigals. We've all been those who asked our Father to give us our share of his gifts, and then went off and used them without regard or gratitude

to him (Luke 15 v 13). And we Christians all have a Father
who kept, and keeps, pursuing:

> *While [the rebellious, prodigal son] was still a long way*
> *off, his father saw him and felt compassion, and ran and*
> *embraced him and kissed him ... the father said to his*
> *servants, "Bring quickly the best robe, and put it on him,*
> *and put a ring on his hand, and shoes on his feet. And*
> *bring the fattened calf and kill it, and let us eat and*
> *celebrate. For this my son was dead, and is alive again;*
> *he was lost, and is found." And they began to celebrate.*
> *(Luke 15 v 20, 22-24)*

Parents must be like the father—like God: looking for,
hoping for, and going out of our way to welcome home an
estranged child, in an embrace that only a parent can give.

Before we finish this chapter, it's vital to remember that
in that same parable, which reminds us of God's wonderful, fatherly love for errant children, there are two sons.
And only one ends the story inside his father's house:

> *Now his older son was in the field, and as he came and*
> *drew near to the house, he heard music and dancing. And*
> *he called one of the servants and asked what these things*
> *meant. And he said to him, "Your brother has come, and*
> *your father has killed the fattened calf, because he has*
> *received him back safe and sound." But he was angry*
> *and refused to go in. His father came out and entreated*
> *him, but he answered his father, "Look, these many years*
> *I have served you, and I never disobeyed your command,*
> *yet you never gave me a young goat, that I might celebrate*
> *with my friends. But when this son of yours came, who*
> *has devoured your property with prostitutes, you killed the*
> *fattened calf for him!" (Luke 15 v 25-30)*

If you, like me, are a Christian parent, we must remember that there is an equal and opposite danger to rebellious living of some kind, and that is proudly obedient living of any kind. The older brother never left home and never did anything wrong—but he did not really love his father, or his brother. We are not seeking to raise children who do the right thing, obey God and their parents, go to church, and know their biblical morality—if that goes along with pride at being better than others, and a sense that they deserve God's approval and blessing more than someone who is living under a trans identity. The thought of raising little Pharisees, who stand on their own sense of moral goodness to look down on others, should grieve us as much as the thought of an obviously rebellious child. Only one may be outside our home, but both are outside their heavenly home.

In that parable, the father loved and moved toward and invited in both of his sons—and we must be like him. In all the ways we talk about this area of gender identity, and in all the ways we talk about all areas of life with our kids, let us be seeking to show, teach, and remind them that they are sinners, who can only ever come home to heaven by God's grace; and let us pray for God's help in raising children who understand that the gospel calls them to obey God even when that is painful, and that the gospel only ever calls them to obey God as a response to his love, not to earn it.

12. TOUGH QUESTIONS

In this chapter, I want to tackle some questions that have not been dealt with in other chapters so far, but which are destined to come up.

The answers are intentionally short, so they are not meant to answer every question fully. The answers are offered in a spirit of humility and unity, and I know that some may answer the questions a little differently than me. These answers are certainly not meant to be the last word on any of these difficult issues.

Q Can someone be transgender and Christian?

Paul's words in 1 Corinthians 6 v 9-11 offer a helpful way to answer this question:

> *Do you not know that the unrighteous will not inherit the kingdom of God? Do not be deceived: neither the sexually immoral, nor idolaters, nor adulterers, nor men who practice homosexuality, nor thieves, nor the greedy, nor drunkards, nor revilers, nor swindlers will inherit the kingdom of God. And such were some of you. But you were*

> *washed, you were sanctified, you were justified in the name*
> *of the Lord Jesus Christ and by the Spirit of our God.*

Paul's words show that there are practices and lifestyles that, if left unrepented of, can prevent someone from inheriting—that is, having a place in—the kingdom of God. To live as a Christian is to accept God's authority over our own.

Transgender identities fall into that category—they are, as we've seen in this book, not compatible with following Christ. A person's gender identity reflects how they define what it means to be a human being. That self-definition will either correspond to God's revelation in his word or it will not. As we have seen, God has created human beings in his own image as male and female. Our identity, therefore, is defined by God in his purposes for his creation and in his new creation in Christ. The design of humanity is purposeful and good, and part of our design is that we are men and women. To deny or overturn that distinction is to nullify God's revelation both in nature and in Scripture. The Bible calls it suppressing the truth in unrighteousness (Romans 1 v 18).

That *doesn't* mean that someone who struggles with gender identity conflicts is not a Christian. As we've seen, all Christians wrestle with life in this fallen world in one way or another. Let me underline that experiencing gender dysphoria does not mean you are not a Christian.

But it does mean that a settled rejection of God's purposes for us as male or female cannot be reconciled with following Christ. Someone can embrace a transgender identity or find their identity in Christ, but not both.

Having said that, it is possible to sin in all kinds of ways in ignorance, rather than willfully and knowingly. A new Christian might not know that they are called to honor their parents, or that lust is sinful. The key is that when they read in Scripture that obedience to God means changing in these areas, they will work to do so, with God's help. Likewise, it would be possible to identify as transgender and also be trusting Christ as Lord because they have not yet realized the implications of the lordship of Christ in this area of their life and identity. As and when they do realize it, a Christian person would change their behavior in this area, with God's help.

Q *Should parents keep kids in a state-run school if those schools promote transgenderism?*

Christians are going to disagree about the wisdom of putting children in a state-run school and whether (and when, and why) to take them out. My own view (for reasons far beyond just the issue of support for transgenderism in schools) is that Christian parents should not put their children in government schools. The increasing support for transgenderism inside public schools is one demonstration of the how problematic such schooling can be for the hearts and minds of young children.

One thing that strikes me as particularly unique about transgenderism as a "political issue" is how it is unlike other disagreements about sexuality within today's culture.

For example, there is debate at the public-school level about sex education—when it should be taught, and how comprehensively. But there is no policy telling students that they're wrong to believe that sex before and outside marriage is wrong. While the law allows for a false belief about how to use our God-given sexuality, it doesn't mandate that every student accept it.

Mainstreaming transgenderism is altogether different. It is designed to stifle debate. The adoption of "gender identity" and transgenderism is going to require active suppression of the view that men and women are intrinsically different and complementary. In other words, active obedience on the part of your child is going to be the government's expectation.

Official government policy on transgenderism in the US faces an uncertain future as a result of the 2016 Presidential election result, but it should not come as a surprise if, someday in the not-too-distant future, official government policy in the US denies that there's anything unique or objective about our biological sex, because it is superseded by the authority of an individual's self-description. This is a comprehensive claim made about human nature. To put it another way, it is a belief statement that brooks no compromise and that will lead the government to seek to correct, rebuke, or silence any dissenting opinion.

So, for example, when Sarah says to her teacher that she thinks it's wrong that Margaret (formerly Michael) is using the same restroom and locker room as she is, what is the teacher to do but correct this new bigotry? Sarah is in violation of government policy, and (according to the government's view) Sarah is committing an act of discrimination by failing to affirm Margaret. To activists, Sarah's concern and failure to conform is a crime far worse than just discrimination, because it's a cause for Margaret's anxiety.

While public education varies from one location to another, the increasing role of the state in education makes it far more likely that all schools will be made to adopt transgender policies uniformly, thus impacting even the most conservative areas.

I think it is unwise to put children into an environment at a young age where they do not have the emotional and psychological maturity to grapple with all that is being taught. It is also problematic to put children into an environment where their views are treated with hostility and made to feel second class. Parents who view state-school education as holding missional possibilities might like to think about the likelihood that a child is more likely to succumb to peer pressure to adapt than to succeed in being an influencer over a large number of children who are being taught beliefs contrary to Christianity.

At the same time, Christians who homeschool or pursue private schooling should not succumb to the mistaken belief that their decision is a sign of Christian maturity over and against other parents who have made a different decision. Nor should parents find self-righteousness in how they educate their children. I know mature and godly Christians who send their kids to government schools, and less mature Christian parents who homeschool. Neither of these paths guarantee Christian faith or maturity in children.

One last thought: if your child is in a state-run school, make sure you are in possession of the facts. Be proactive in asking teachers what your child will be taught about the whole area of human identity and sexuality, and when and how. Find out the school's restroom policies. Know whether you have the right to withdraw your child from particular lessons that touch on these areas. And think, pray and discuss ahead of time what your "red lines" are—in what circumstances would you decide that godly parenting means withdrawing your child(ren) from the school?

Q *What should church elders/leaders do if a congregation member asks for their child to be identified as the opposite gender (or neither gender)?*

Each situation is unique because each child is unique. Pastors and/or elders will want to meet with the parent(s) and listen well and humbly to them, as well as discussing with them the Bible's view on sex and gender.

It's important to remember that the same request could be made with very different motivations. For example, a parent may hold to the Bible's teaching but be trying to parent wisely a teenager who is feeling suicidal, and so their request is based on a desire to enable their child to feel able to keep coming to church without it increasing their temptation to self-harm, while the parent seeks to model and teach loving biblical standards in the home. That parent requires very different help than a parent who is wanting to ignore and deny God's word because they think that is in their child's best interest.

But whatever the situation in the home may be, pastors and elders should say they'll be unable to comply with this parent's request, or to ask anyone else in the church to do this, because it goes against what the Bible teaches about who this child is. But if the situation were the first one in the paragraph above, this non-compliance needs to be accompanied by empathy, by prayer, and by putting structures in place to support and counsel the parent(s) and (if he/she is willing) the child.

Remember that whatever the motivation of the parent, in such a meeting (or meetings—don't assume one meeting is sufficient), your tone matters.

If the parent is opposed to the Bible's teaching (rather than in agreement with it but struggling to know how best to love their suffering child), and refuses to change their mind, I'd see this as an issue of church discipline, because the parent is publicly living in rejection of God's word. Of course, the manner and means of church discipline will vary between churches.

Q *Should I mind if people who are biologically the other sex are in my restroom? What if it's my kids in the restroom?*

Each person will respond differently to these challenges, based in large part on our level of discomfort at sharing a restroom with someone of the opposite sex.

But in general, restroom policies separate men and women based on privacy concerns. Individuals of the same biological sex share the same anatomy. Sharing the restroom with those who are of the same sex and who have the same anatomy prevents the embarrassment or vulnerability that comes from the possibility of viewing the opposite sex in a state of undress. For the sake of protecting women from sexual assault or the fear of it and to prevent men from viewing, or being in close proximity to, women in a private situation, restroom policies are wise to base access upon biological sex distinction.

When it comes to children, I think it is extremely unwise to put children in a situation where they could be wantonly exposed to the genitalia of the opposite sex or where their own genitalia could be exposed to an adult member of the opposite sex. Parents should not interpret that last sentence to mean that a son or daughter's exposure to an undressed parent is equally wrong or harmful. What a child sees inside a house with a family member in the course of normal family life is a separate issue than government policy making opposite-sex exposure inside a public restroom the norm. Cultures will vary in the level of awkwardness someone may feel at seeing a member of the opposite sex who they don't know in a state of undress or using the restroom. But those variations do not overrule the safety and privacy concerns of parents, who may—and should feel able to— strongly protest such a circumstance.

Q *If a church is told to provide restrooms for transgendered people in its buildings, should it do so in submission to the authorities, or should it refuse to do so?*

In order to be compassionate and welcoming, I think it would be appropriate and accommodating to voluntarily designate one single-stall restroom in the church as open to all genders.

If the state mandates at least one single-stall restroom open to all genders, then I think it is up to church leadership to determine the scope of their obedience.

But if the state insists upon multiple-occupant restrooms being open to all genders as a matter of obeying public accommodation law, then the church should disobey the governing authorities and challenge such a policy in court. The church should understand that the government does not have the authority or competence to decree what the church's internal policies must be related to restroom access inside the church—especially considering that a church's bathroom-access policy will be based on prior commitments which the church has to biblical teaching on sex and gender. At least in the United States, churches have great authority over how they govern their internal policies.

Q *Is taking hormones to manage dysphoria ever appropriate?*

There is likely to be disagreement among Christians on this subject, and this is a very short answer to a fairly complex question. My own position is that any effort or action taken to suppress the truth of our natural biology, or to reverse our natural biology, runs contrary to God's word.

The intention of hormone therapy is to interrupt or thwart natural development. Such therapy is aimed at contradicting otherwise healthy bodily development based on the view of someone's mind and/or feelings. People who experience bouts of gender dysphoria are not necessarily destined to experience those bouts forever. So it's unwise (as well as going against God's word) to take drastic, irreversible action to seek to "fix" what may have been temporary.

Using anti-depressants seems a far more reasonable and less invasive way to treat individuals who experience depression and anxiety that stem from gender dysphoria.

Q *Shouldn't we just focus on sins that are actually harming people (murder, adultery, etc.)? Transgenderism is harmless, isn't it?*

Much of the answer depends on how we define "harm."

In one sense, identifying as transgender does not "harm" someone in the way that stealing or adultery does.

But "harm" means much more than transactional harm between two persons, because "harm" runs much deeper than what's on the surface. Individuals can think that an action of theirs produces no apparent harm, but unless they have perfect knowledge (which none of us do), they cannot know that it does not.

It is possible to harm yourself without realizing it. An addict alone in his basement is doing harm to himself even though no third party is being harmed, and even though he may not accept that he is harming himself.

Someone addicted to pornography is doing harm to himself by needing ever more graphic and violent portrayals of sexual acts to be sexually entertained. Moreover, long-term use of pornography inhibits the ability of people addicted to porn to have relationships with the opposite sex—so they are also harming any future spouse of theirs.

Harm as it relates to someone identifying as transgender has to do with considering whether identifying as transgender promotes lasting health and flourishing. It it not right or good for Christians or churches to promote, or through silence fail to oppose, a worldview that undermines God's good purpose to bless people individually and in society, which leaves people outside the kingdom of God, and which tells hurting people that invasive medical surgery will be the path to fulfillment when we know (both statistically and from God's word) that it will not be. It is right and good for Christians and churches lovingly and gently to promote truth, to point to Christ as the means of entering the kingdom, and to point to God's creation plan as the way to live well in this world as part of that kingdom.

It is worth also saying that often, embracing a transgender identity does hurt other people. If your highest "value" is to avoid doing anything that harms others, then it is worth considering the third parties (parents, spouses, children, siblings) who are hurt by someone's rejection of their birth sex and their upbringing or their marriage vows. The argument that "It doesn't hurt anyone" often ends up simply being "It doesn't hurt anyone who agrees with me," which is not the same thing.

Q *Is it true that Christian teaching is harmful because not affirming a person's transgender identity leads to depression and higher rates of suicide?*

Kids and adults struggling to come to terms with their identities may well fear rejection if their parents are Christians or if they are surrounded by a Christian community. We cannot ignore or deny that there are young people who commit suicide or seriously harm themselves because their rigidly religious parents have condemned them or kicked them out of the house. We have to make sure that as individuals and churches we are welcoming, listening, and compassionate (see chapters eight and ten), and acknowledge that we have not always been those things.

But is it then reasonable to conclude that Christian beliefs must put kids who experience gender dysphoria (or, for that matter, same-sex attraction) in danger? Absolutely not.

Quite the opposite is true. It is a fundamental command of Christianity to love others unconditionally. We are called to love even those who insult and hate us. With God's help, we will love our children, even if they challenge our values. Think of the story of the prodigal son and his boundlessly gracious father. If we are truly to live as Christians, we can only cast ourselves on the Father's loving forgiveness and extend the same grace to others.

The Christian gospel offers a third possibility for parents to hold out to children who are struggling with their sexuality to hold out to them—the life of cross-carrying faithfulness, and of finding joy in the struggle. Christianity, while never promising complete liberation from someone's battles with sin in this life, liberates individuals to experience their truest self, as made in the image of God.

It is an emotionally charged accusation to suppose that disagreement with any given identity or feeling is the cause of someone's emotional stress. And it raises an important counter-question: is the emotional distress caused from identifying as transgender the result of not being affirmed, or is it a feature of the underlying emotional and mental difficulties that come with gender dysphoria, which are not solved by embracing a transgender identity?

Your presupposition about whether transgenderism is good or not good will tend to dictate how you read the statistics that are available. Someone who affirms or promotes embracing a transgender identity will assume the distress is caused by societal rejection; someone who believes transgender is not in line with God's good purposes will tend to argue that the distress is caused by the dysphoria and responding to it by adopting a transgender identity.

From a biblical-worldview perspective, it seems far more likely (albeit that it's unpopular to say) that emotional and psychological distress stem from gender dysphoria, not from the failure to feel affirmed by one's community. If we believe that it is in living under God's good rule, in line with how he created us to flourish, that leads to greater fulfillment and wholeness, then we have also to believe that it would be harmful not to speak God's word into this area, hard though it may be to say and for people to hear.

Q *How should we think about pronouns?*

It's very common to hear debates about pronoun usage. For example, should you call a transgender male "he" (as they identify themselves) or "she" (since they are biologically female)?

Christians disagree—hopefully charitably—about pronoun usage.

Some think that as a personal courtesy, you should refer to a transgender person by their preferred pronoun as a way to extend courtesy in hopes of developing a relationship in which biblical truth can eventually be shared. Others think that it is wrong to inject further confusion into a person's situation by referring to them with a pronoun that is not aligned with their biological sex. Some Christians argue that referring to a person by their preferred pronoun furthers the deception and delusion within a person's mind. Seen this way, calling a biological male "she" is to bear false witness.

My own position is that if a transgender person comes to your church, it is fine to refer to them by their preferred pronoun. While a person may act out of the best intention in thinking they should confront a person's pronoun usage immediately upon meeting them, or refuse to comply with their preference, this could result in unnecessary provocation and confrontation. If and when this person desires greater involvement or membership in the church—or if, for example, a biological male wants to attend a woman's Bible study—a church leader will need to meet with them and talk about how they identify and what faithful church involvement and membership will look like, including (but not limited to!) which pronoun they are referred to by.

The best solution is to avoid pronouns altogether if possible. Calling a person by their legal name or preferred name is more acceptable because names are not objectively gendered, but change from culture to culture.

Q *What about people who are born intersex?*

There are several questions that come under this headline question. Are intersex people really any different than those who feel themselves to be transgender or non-binary? Doesn't the existence of intersex people mean that "male and female he created them" isn't an absolute statement?

"Intersex" is a term that describes a range of conditions affecting the development of the human reproductive system. These disorders of sex development result in atypical reproductive anatomy. Some intersex persons are born with ambiguous genitalia, which makes sex determination at birth very difficult.

Many link the existence of intersex people with transgenderism. The argument goes thus: some people are born intersex, so their gender is unclear from their anatomy; and some people are born transgender, so their gender is also unclear from their anatomy. Further, intersex, it's argued, proves that gender is not a binary, but a spectrum.

But these are very different categories. Those who identify as transgender are not dealing with ambiguity concerning their biological sex. Transgenderism refers to the variety of ways in which some people feel that their gender identity is out of sync with their biological sex. Transgender identities are built on the assumption that biological sex is known and clear—and then rejected. Medical intervention for intersex people is aimed at enabling them to live out the sex and gender that they were born with, but which is physically unclear one way or another. Medical intervention for those identifying as transgender is aimed at the very opposite—at obscuring the sex they were born with.

Intersexuality and transgenderism are apples and oranges. Those who are pushing the gender revolution have an interest in confusing the categories. But intersex conditions do not disprove the sexual binary. This does not nullify or invalidate the scriptural truth that "male and female he created them" because intersex conditions are a deviation from the binary norm, not the establishment of a new norm. To think in biblical language, what we are seeing here is an aspect of creation that has been marred by the fall—a deviation from a norm that reaffirms that a norm exists in the first place.

But a critical reader may respond, "How can you say it is possible to deviate from the binary norm in the case of intersex people, but not possible for transgender people to legitimately differ from that norm?" The answer is that in cases involving intersex persons, there are body, chromosomal, and/or anatomical abnormalities that are medically diagnosable and empirically verifiable. No such parallel exists in the case of transgenderism, because no definitive conclusion as to its cause has been determined; nor is it empirically verifiable—it's a psychological construct. A transgender individual who identifies as a member of the sex different than their biological sex does not become an authentic member of the opposite sex just because they will such a change. While dysphoria is a real phenomenon, that reality does not in itself make it possible for someone to actually be a member of the opposite sex.

There is a clear category-difference between being intersex and being transgender. Being born intersex often (though not always) brings its own share of questions, issues, and pain. Parents of children born intersex need churches not to confuse the decisions they may make (or decide to delay until their child is older) with the decisions being made by those who identify as transgender. And those parents and their children need those who aim to push the transgender cause not to attempt to yoke them in service to that cause.

13. OPEN HANDS

In chapter two, I made a fleeting reference to a particular detail of Caitlyn Jenner's famous appearance on the cover of *Vanity Fair*. It was this: there were no hands visible in the photo. They were out of shot, placed behind Jenner's back.

Why mention this again at the end of the book? It's because the absence of Jenner's hands from the photo was surely intentional.

A blog post by a photographer went viral after the *Vanity Fair* release:

> *"One of my mentors has always said, a good photograph should stand on its own, meaning it alone tells its story and the backstory is irrelevant. If you accept this, what I see when I look at this image is a badly posed person looking awkwardly at the camera … I am confused—why are the hands hidden? The very masculine shoulders, arms, and legs suggest to me that this is a drag queen—notwithstanding the breasts, a flare to the hips, and a lack of an Adam's apple, as I know all of that can be achieved through Photoshop—and that the photographer just did not know what to do with large, mannish hands. And so [he] told the subject to hide them."* [30]

---

30 www.stephaniericherphoto.com/blog/2015/6/3/on-caitlyn-jenners-vanity-fair-cover-shot.

Look at your hands right now. If you're a man, it's likely that your hands are longer and thicker than a woman's. There's a ruggedness about a man's hands that make them better suited to physical labor. If you're a woman, it's very likely that your hands are smaller than a man's. A woman's hands are more delicate. The bones are smaller. The knuckles don't protrude quite like a man's. They are not as strong or as hairy as a man's hand.

Why finish this book talking about hands? Because the lack of hands on the cover of *Vanity Fair*—the cover that has perhaps done more than anything else to make gender transition mainstream and attractive—tells us a great deal not only about Jenner's struggles for self-acceptance but about the very nature of the transgender debate.

The fact is that in that photo shoot, Jenner went to every possible effort to demonstrate femininity, and took every step possible to assert sex appeal as a woman—eyelashes, breasts, facial work. But the hands did not, could not, follow. And that tells us something: Our existence simply cannot be remade or recast without remnants of our true self somehow remaining.

We can try to tamper with God's design, but how he made the world and each of us continues, even when it goes against our will, to shine through. Jenner had to hide his hands from the camera, because Jenner's male-born hands are a reminder that whatever perception we have of ourselves, there are objective traits to our existence that tell the truth about who we really are. Our hands don't tell us everything about who we are. But they do remind us about how we have been made.

All of us try to hide parts of our existence—whether physical or emotional. All of us feel some sense of shame about some of the realities of who we are. We humans have been hiding since the Garden of Eden. And since that moment, we've also been craving for a stable sense of identity and a deep knowledge of acceptance.

Which takes us to another pair of hands.

> *Now Thomas, one of the twelve, called the Twin, was not with them when Jesus came [after he had risen from the dead]. So the other disciples told him, "We have seen the Lord." But he said to them, "Unless I see in his hands the mark of the nails, and place my finger into the mark of the nails, and place my hand into his side, I will never believe."*
>
> *Eight days later, his disciples were inside again, and Thomas was with them. Although the doors were locked, Jesus came and stood among them and said, "Peace be with you." Then he said to Thomas, "Put your finger here, and see my hands; and put out your hand, and place it in my side. Do not disbelieve, but believe." Thomas answered him, "My Lord and my God!" (John 20 v 24-28)*

Jesus proved his resurrection to his doubting disciples by holding out his hands—real, resurrected hands, with real, nail-caused scars.

Jesus' hands were, and are, scarred from the cross, where he took the brokenness of the world upon himself in order to redeem his creation. His hands were, and are, a reminder that he was broken so that you and I can be re-stored—mind, heart, and body. We have a God with scars, who knows what brokenness feels like and who offers a future of real and lasting wholeness, beyond all of the frustration and all of the pain.

And he did not, and does not, hide those hands behind his back.

He held them out to Thomas to prove who he was—the loving, suffering Savior—and to ask him to come to him, and believe in him, and follow him. He holds them out to people still today. He has nothing to hide, and everything to give.

The hiding of Caitlyn Jenner's masculine hands show that the way through and out of gender dysphoria cannot be to transition our gender. The holding out of Jesus' scarred hands show that there is a way through and out of all our struggles and brokenness. It is to come to him, and to find forgiveness from him, transformation through him, and forever with him. His words in Matthew 11 v 28 are to us, whoever we are, as he invites us to come to him, and beckons us on as we follow him:

> *Come to me, all who labor and are heavy laden, and I will give you rest.*

APPENDIX

Here is a list of many of the terms that form part of the language used in discussion about gender identity, and what they mean, courtesy of Joe Carter.[31]

Agender — A term for people who consider themselves to be without a gender ("a–" meaning "without"). Sometimes referred to as *genderless, genderfree, non-gendered,* or *ungendered.*

Androphilia — A term used to refer to sexual attraction to men or masculinity that can be used as an alternative to a gender-binary heterosexual or homosexual orientation. (See also: *Gynephilia.*)

Bigender — A person who has two gender identities or expressions, either at the same time, at different times, or in different social situations. (See also: *Genderfluid.*)

Binary — A term for people who associate with typical male or female behaviors. The opposite of non-binary or genderqueer. (See also: *Cisgender.*)

Bisexual — A person who is attracted to two sexes or two genders, but not necessarily simultaneously or equally. Although the term used to be defined as a person who is

---

31 This list originally appeared at: www.thegospelcoalition.org/article/from-agender-to-ze-a-glossary-for-the-gender-identity-revolution.

attracted to both genders or both sexes, that has been replaced by the number two (2) since the LGBTQ community believes there are not only two sexes or two genders but multiple gender identities. Within the LGBTQ community, a person who is sexually attracted to more than two biological sexes or gender identities is often referred to as *pansexual* or *omnisexual.*

Butch — A term used by the LGBTQ community to refer to masculine gender expression or gender identity. A non-binary butch is a person who holds a non-binary gender identity and a butch gender expression, or claiming butch as an identity outside of the gender binary. (See also: *Femme.*)

Cisgender — A term used to refer to people who have a match between the gender they were assigned at birth, their bodies, and their personal identity. Cisgender is often used within the LGBTQ community to refer to people who are not transgender. (In general, Christians should avoid using this term since it implies that cisgender and transgender are equally normative, i.e. the opposite of *heteronormative.*)

Femme — A term used by the LGBTQ community to refer to feminine gender expression or gender identity. A non-binary femme is a person who holds a non-binary gender identity and a femme gender expression, or claiming femme as an identity outside of the gender binary. (See also: *Butch.*)

Gay — Until the mid-20th century, the term gay was originally used to refer to feelings of being "carefree," "happy," or "bright and showy," though it also added, in the late 17th century, the meaning "addicted to pleasures and dissipations" implying that a person was uninhibited by moral constraints. In the 1960s, the term began to be used in reference to people attracted to members of the same sex, who often found the term "homosexual" to be too clinical or critical. Currently, the term "gay" is used to refer to men attracted to people who identify as men, though it is also used colloquially as an umbrella term to include all LGBTQ people. (The Gay & Lesbian Alliance Against Defamation considers the term "homosexual" to be offensive and recommends that journalists use the term "gay.")

Gender identity — A term used to refer to an individual's personal sense of identity as masculine or feminine, or some combination of each. The LGBTQ community and their allies consider gender to be a trait that exists along a continuum and is not inherently rooted in biology or physical expressions.

Genderfluid — A term used for people who prefer to be flexible about their gender identity. They may fluctuate between genders (a man one minute, a woman the next, a third sex later in the day) or express multiple gender identities at the same time.

Genderqueer — An umbrella term for gender identities that are not exclusively masculine or feminine. Sometimes referred to as *non-binary, gender-expansive, pangender, polygender*. (See also: *Bigender, Trigender.*)

Gynephilia — A term used to refer to sexual attraction to women or femininity that can be used as an alternative to a gender-binary homosexual or heterosexual orientation. (See also: *Androphilia.*)

Heteronormative — Popularized in the early 1990s in Queer Theory, the term refers to lifestyle norms that hold that people fall into distinct and complementary genders (man and woman) based on biology, with natural roles in life that may or may not be socially constructed. Heteronomativity presumes that heterosexual behavior is the norm for sexual practices and that sexual and marital relations are only fitting between a man and a woman. (The Christian worldview is heteronormative. The Bible clearly presents gender and heterosexual sex within the bounds of marriage as part of the goodness of God's created order.)

Intergender — A term for people who have a gender identity in the middle between the binary genders of female and male, and who may be a mix of both.

Intersex — Intersex is a general term for a variety of physical conditions in which a person is born with a reproductive or sexual anatomy that doesn't seem to fit the typical definitions of female or male. The variations in sex characteristics may include chromosomes, gonads, or genitals that do not allow an individual to be distinctly identified as male or female. Intersex is a physical condition while transgender is a psychological condition. The vast majority of people with intersex conditions identify as male or female rather than transgender or transsexual. (The term "hermaphrodite" is now considered outdated, inaccurate, and offensive as a reference to people who are intersex.)

Lesbian — The term most widely used in the English language to describe sexual and romantic attraction between people who identify as females. The word is derived from the name of the Greek island of Lesbos, home to Sappho (6th-century BC), a female poet who proclaimed her love for girls. The term "gay and lesbian" became more popular in the 1970s as a way of acknowledging the two broad sexual-political communities that were part of the gay-liberation movement.

LGBTQ — An initialism that collectively refers to the lesbian, gay, bisexual, transgender, and queer communities. In use since the 1990s, the term is an adaptation of the initialism LGB, which itself started replacing the phrase "gay community" beginning in the mid-to-late 1980s. The initialism has become mainstream as a self-designation and has been adopted by the majority of sexuality- and gender-identity-based community centers and media in the United States. Along with LGBTQ, other letters are sometimes added. Other variants include: an extra "Q" for "questioning"; "U" for "unsure"; "C" for "curious"; an "I" for "intersex"; another "T" for "transsexual" or "transvestite"; another "T," "TS," or "2" for "Two–Spirit" persons; an "A" or "SA" for "straight allies"; or an "A" for "asexual"; "P" for "pansexual" or "polyamorous"; "H" for "HIV-affected"; and "O" for "other."

Queer — An umbrella term for sexual and gender minorities that are not heterosexual, heteronormative, or gender-binary. The term is still controversial, even within the LGBTQ community, because it was once used as a slur against homosexuals until it was re-appropriated in the 1990s. The range of what "queer" includes varies, though in addition to referring to LGBT-identifying people, it can also encompass: *pansexual, pomosexual, intersexual, genderqueer, asexual,* and *autosexual* people, and even gender-normative heterosexuals whose sexual orientations or activities place them outside the heterosexual-defined mainstream, e.g. BDSM practitioners, or polyamorous persons. (In academia, the term "queer" and its verbal use, "queering," indicate the study of literature, academic fields, and other social and cultural areas from a non-heteronormative perspective.)

Man/Woman — In LGBTQ parlance, terms that refer to a person's chosen gender identity, regardless of biological characteristics.

Non-binary — See *genderqueer.*

Sex — The term was previously used to distinguish between the physical identification assigned as at birth (e.g. male, female, or intersex). It's now used by LGBTQ groups and their allies as synonymous with a self-chosen gender identity.

Third gender — A concept in which individuals are categorized, either by themselves or by society, as neither man nor woman (though not necessarily intersex). Sometimes also called "third sex" or "othergender." (See also: *Queer.*)

Transgenderism — An umbrella term for the state or condition of identifying or expressing a gender identity that does not match a person's physical/genetic sex. Transgender is independent of sexual orientation, and those who self-identify as transgender may consider themselves to be *heterosexual, homosexual, bisexual, pansexual, polysexual,* or *asexual.* Approximately 700,000 individuals in the United States identify as transgender.

Trans man — A transgender person who was born a female but claims the gender identity of a man (i.e. a biological female who identifies as a male).

Transsexual — A narrower term used to refer to people who identify as the opposite of their birth-gender designation, regardless of whether they have undergone or intend to undergo hormone-replacement therapy and/or sex-re-assignment surgery.

Trans woman — A transgender person who was born a male but who claims the gender identity of a woman (i.e. a biological male who identifies as a female).

Transvestite — A person who cross-dresses, or dresses in clothes of the opposite sex, though they may not identify with or want to be the opposite gender. (All transexuals are transgender, but transvestites do not necessarily fall into either of the other categories.)

Trigender — A term for a non-binary (i.e. genderqueer) gender identity in which one shifts between or among the behaviors of three genders. These genders may include male, female, and third gender (e.g. *genderless, non-gender, polygender,* etc).

Two-spirit — A term used by some Native American LGBTQ activists for people who posses qualities of both binary genders.

Ze — A gender-neutral pronoun used to replace he/she. (Sometimes spelled as *Xe*.)

ACKNOWLEDGMENTS

O ne of the great evidences of grace in my life is the friends that God has given me. No less have they been a blessing to me than through the writing of this book.

Andrew Wolgemuth, my literary agent, is owed tremendous thanks for helping me navigate through areas of publishing that are foreign to me.

Many individuals read portions of the manuscript and provided helpful feedback: Lindsay Swartz, Dan Darling, Matthew Arbo, and Catherine Parks. Mentors like Denny Burk provided helpful feedback along the way. There were numerous times throughout the writing of this book when I would explain my thinking on a subject to him and he would helpfully challenge it to greater depths. Phillip Bethancourt, who is both my boss and one of the greatest friends a man could ask for, provided encouragement during the project, and gave me great freedom in my schedule to write. I must also recognize Russell Moore, for various thoughts expressed in this book are a reflection of his impact on my thinking as a result of my working alongside him since 2013 and knowing him as a friend since 2008.

I also have to say thank you to my friend and fellow church member Trillia Newbell. She gave my name to the publisher and the rest was history. I've told Trillia that her assistance in helping match my publisher, The Good Book Company, with a young Christian ethicist interested in transgender issues was an answer to a prayer that my family had been praying.

David Closson helped me with research. David is a sharp thinker for his age, and that is only complemented by his eagerness to serve.

My experience of working with The Good Book Company has been terrific. Carl Laferton is a brilliant editor, and frustratingly effective at playing "devil's advocate." Joking aside, Carl's editorial feedback was immensely helpful, and his eloquent, simple prose helped bring concision and elegance to someone prone to academic verbosity. Brad Byrd, the North American Director at TGBC, was also a helpful voice through the planning and execution of this book. To my fellow central-Illinoisan, thank you for being a wise voice seeking to amplify an important topic to the church.

Finally, I must give thanks to my wife, Christian, and our two daughters, Caroline and Catherine. Christian endured this project alongside me as early mornings of work on this book and on my doctorate led to many nights of me falling asleep much too early. She and my family are a source of boundless joy.

thegoodbook
COMPANY

Opening up the Bible

At The Good Book Company, we are dedicated to helping Christians and local churches grow. We believe that God's growth process always starts with hearing clearly what he has said to us through his timeless word—the Bible.

Ever since we opened our doors in 1991, we have been striving to produce resources that honor God in the way the Bible is used. We have grown to become an international provider of user-friendly resources to the Christian community, with believers of all backgrounds and denominations using our Bible studies, books, evangelistic resources, DVD-based courses and training events.

We want to equip ordinary Christians to live for Christ day by day, and churches to grow in their knowledge of God, their love for one another, and the effectiveness of their outreach.

Call us for a discussion of your needs or visit one of our local websites for more information on the resources and services we provide.

Your friends at The Good Book Company

NORTH AMERICA   thegoodbook.com   866 244 2165
UK & EUROPE   thegoodbook.co.uk   0333 123 0880
AUSTRALIA   thegoodbook.com.au   (02) 9564 3555
NEW ZEALAND   thegoodbook.co.nz   (+64) 3 343 2463

WWW.CHRISTIANITYEXPLORED.ORG
Our partner site is a great place for those exploring the Christian faith, with a clear explanation of the good news, powerful testimonies and answers to difficult questions.